P9-DIB-574

TOUCHSTONE

The Complete Plays of Vladimir Mayakovsky

Translated by
GUY DANIELS

With an introduction by
ROBERT PAYNE

A TOUCHSTONE BOOK
Published by Simon and Schuster

A Touchstone Book
Published by Simon and Schuster
Rockefeller Center, 630 Fifth Avenue
New York, New York 10020

SBN 671-20926-4
Manufactured in the United States of America

2 3 4 5 6 7 8 9 10

TRANSLATOR'S DEDICATION

TO

Frances Keene,

donna di piagente core

Contents

Introduction *1*

Vladimir Mayakovsky, A Tragedy *19*

Mystery-Bouffe *39*

The Bedbug *141*

The Bathhouse *197*

Notes *265*

The Complete Plays of Vladimir Mayakovsky

VLADIMIR MAYAKOVSKY

Who is he?
Who is that free spirit?
Who is he —
that nameless one?
Who is he
with no country of his own?
Why did he come?
What prophecies did he utter?
— *Mystery-Bouffe*

I

Long before he died, on April 14, 1930, the figure of Mayakovsky had assumed legendary proportions. He seemed not to belong to the real world, but to another world where everything was larger, louder, brighter, more fiercely energetic, and more beautiful. It was a world of elemental forces shimmering with the colors of the rainbow, where the sun never set and no winter fell. In that world he was perpetually striding forward, his head tossed back, his yellow shirt open at the neck, his voice shouting above the thunder. He was a giant in seven-league boots, and like the ancient folk hero Ilya Muromets, he was so careless of his power that he was scarcely aware of the enemies he was treading underfoot.

Out of that ancient legendary world where he was at home, Mayakovsky sometimes gave the impression of hurtling violently like a rocket or a celestial steam engine into the everyday world, scattering everything before him. Not long ago a Chinese poet described Peking man emerging out of the red earth to terrify the present inhabitants of China. So with Mayakovsky. An elemental, primitive force surged through him, and finally shattered him. He was at home in the tempests and the snowstorms, and he was never comfortable unless the lightning was playing about him.

Such men do not appear frequently, and they have no imitators. In the history of Russian poetry Mayakovsky stands alone, not only because he had no poetical ancestors and created an entirely new form of poetry, but also because he emerged at a time when Russia was herself primitive, chaotic, and convulsive, pouring out blood and energy on a scale undreamed of until this time. The whirlwind of Mayakovsky met the whirlwind of the Revolution head on, and if they sometimes seemed to be the same whirlwind, if they often appeared to be moving in the same direction, they were nevertheless separate and distinct. Sometimes he drew the Revolution round him like a cloak, but he could just as well walk without it.

Everything about him was larger than life: his voice, his manners, his arrogance, his appetites, his gifts. He wrote poetry as though he were hammering rivets into sheet iron, and he conducted his life as though he had a thousand lives to spare. When he painted a portrait, he would search for the largest canvas he could lay his hands on, and hurl on it the brightest and purest colors from his palette, and in the same way, when he wrote poetry, he would search for the brightest and largest words, and hurl them down on the largest sheet of paper available, always taking care to give the words space to breathe in. There was nothing niggardly about him; he poured out poetry in a torrential and undeviating flow, and it is possible that he never knew whether he was writing at the top of his genius or at the lowest pitch of his talent. That he was born and died seemed the least important thing about him; it is not the birth or the death of a cyclone that one remembers. One remembers the destructive path and the raging of the heavens.

When he first appeared on the literary scene, he was already fully formed, possessing an authentic voice which was to remain largely unchanged for a quarter of a century. He called himself a "futurist," but that was merely his way of saying that he came from the remote past. He was tall, heavily built, with a large mouth, brilliant blue-gray eyes, a heavy jaw, the look of a peasant who had wandered out of Bohemia. His father was a forester in Georgia, who died when Mayakovsky was young, leaving the family destitute; he was about thirteen when he first became a Bolshevik, serving as a courier and gunrunner, and he was fifteen when he had his first taste of prison. In 1913, when he was twenty, he wrote, produced, and acted in his first dramatic work. Characteristically he called it *Vladimir Mayakovsky, A Tragedy.*

He made no attempt to disguise the theme of the play, which was the celebration of his own poetic genius and apotheosis as the divine poet crowned with laurel leaves, ascending to heaven while intoning his own name. The naked exuberance, the ferocity of the self-adulation, and the brilliance of the imagery seemed to indicate that he had reached the stage of egotistic romanticism beyond which it was impossible to go. In time he was to show that this was the merest beginning. He later extended the range of his exuberance and self-admiration until they encompassed vast unexplored regions of his ego, and he continued to display an extraordinary power to invent images which sent the mind reeling.

Vladimir Mayakovsky, A Tragedy was a tragedy only in the sense that the *Divina Commedia* was a comedy: there was simply no available poetic description for it. Most of the characters, even those who offer tribute to Mayakovsky, were Mayakovsky. The Man Without a Head, the Man with One Ear, the Man with One Eye and One Leg, the Man with Two Kisses, the Man with a Long Drawn-out Face, the Conventional Young Man, and the Old Man with Scrawny Black Cats were all Mayakovsky in his various manifestations, and there is some question whether The Enormous Woman, fifteen to twenty feet tall, was not a projection of the Mayakovsky who in his final appearance wishes he had breasts large enough to feed everyone. Even the Woman with a Tiny Tear, the Woman with a Tear, and the Woman with a Great Big Tear may be regarded as projections of Mayakovsky's devouring self-pity. "Things must be destroyed," says the Old Man with Scrawny Black Cats, and since "things" includes "people," who are no more than bells on the duncecap of God, the poet seems inclined to view the prospect of universal destruction with jaunty indifference. His true habitation is not the world but abstract Time, which buries all things in its capacious belly. As for love, this is just one more of the encumbrances which must be destroyed. "If you had loved as I have loved, you would murder love," says the Man with a Long Drawn-out Face, offering as an alternative the promise of celestial debauchery with "the shaggy, sweat-dripping sky and the milky-innocent stars." It is an unlikely promise, and Mayakovsky does not pursue it farther, although at intervals he will introduce the vast abstractions of Sky, Space, Time, Universes. Time is his special bugbear, for he knows that Time alone can destroy him; and in a strange and wonderful image the Man with One Eye and One Leg describes the ultimate terror:

> . . . the snouts of the years that came crawling out;
> on the foreheads of cities
> anger swelled up into rivers
> of thousand-mile-long-veins.
> Slowly,
> in terror,
> arrows of hair
> rose up on the bald pate of Time.

Not all of the play, of course, reaches that height of terror. Sometimes the game is played as a farce, with Mayakovsky clowning his various roles and turning metaphysical cartwheels. He was an intellectual anarchist, and he soon tired of those huge and ponderous images set in the warring heavens. There is, for example, the question of supplying sufficient electricity to run the tramways. The Old Man with Scrawny Black Cats suggests that it could be done by stroking the backs of his cats and catching the electricity:

. . . streetcars will start off in a rush;
the flame of wicks
will glow in the night like triumphant banners.
The world, in gay greasepaint, will stir into action;
the flowers in the windows will strut, peacock bright;
people will travel on rails –
always trailed
by cats, more cats, lots of black cats!
We'll pin the sun on the gowns of our sweethearts;
we'll adorn them with glittering brooches of stars.
Leave your apartments!
Go stroke cats –
stroke cats that are black and scrawny!

The cats, you observe, have nothing whatsoever to do with the tragedy of Mayakovsky, who is merely improvising in the intervals of superintending his flock of worshipers; and it is precisely these improvisations which give pleasure to the reader who, without them, would find the going hard and the rewards uncertain. Happily, nine-tenths of the time Mayakovsky forgets to posture in front of distorting mirrors, and displays a gift for comic improvisation. Nevertheless, the mirrors are always waiting for him. So, too, are those vast cosmological arguments which continually tempt him to measure himself against the heavens. The comic interlude with the cats is inevitably interrupted with some pious nonsense about pinning the sun on the gowns of our sweethearts and adorning them with glittering brooches of stars. At such times he was no longer fooling; he was merely imitating himself.

When Mayakovsky first acted out the part of Mayakovsky on the stage of the Luna Park Theater in St. Petersburg, he was still little known. He had been writing poetry for a little more than a year under the guidance of his friend, the painter David Burlyuk, who on the evidence of a single poem assured him that he was a genius. *Vladimir Mayakovsky, A Tragedy* was an act of such prodigious effrontery that it brought him to public attention. He was sometimes booed, but never shouted off the stage, for he had a louder voice than all the combined voices of his audience. He took the play on tour, and learned to shout down hecklers in all the dialects of provincial Russia. On that small stage in Luna Park, against a backcloth depicting a spider's web of streets which he had painted himself, he had his beginnings as an actor; and he was to continue to act out the role of the tragedian Mayakovsky as long as he lived.

II

When the Bolshevik Revolution broke out, most of the Russian poets and novelists welcomed it. With the emergence of Lenin, the long years of stagnation came to an end, and they saw the promise of a new birth, a new dispensation of time in which Russia would surge forward, free of the accumulated rubbish left by centuries of misrule. In those early months of revolution there were few intellectuals who guessed that an even more bureaucratic and tyrannical form of government would be imposed upon them.

Mayakovsky did not so much welcome the October Revolution as embrace it ecstatically and joyfully. Although he was and remained an intellectual anarchist with no understanding of Marxism, and therefore with no understanding of the kind of society which the new regime was planning to impose on Russia, he threw himself wholeheartedly into propaganda work for the Bolsheviks. He never became a member of the Party: instead he became its most skilled propagandist and most tireless advocate. What he admired above all was the ruthless energy of the Bolsheviks, their promise to build a state in which the mighty were humbled and the poor were glorified.

The Party needed him. Nowhere else could there be found a man who was simultaneously a loud-voiced poet, a playwright, an actor, a *metteur en scène,* a painter, a cartoonist, a lampooner, a vigorous speaker, and a confirmed demagogue. Mayakovsky could improvise on any subject – even on Bolshevism. Anatol Lunacharsky, the perpetual Commissar for Education, gave him a free hand, forgiving him his egocentricities because he had an instinctive feeling for propaganda: while celebrating himself, Mayakovsky enjoyed the spectacle of himself against the fiery backcloth of the Revolution. He spoke like thunder, and the Revolution needed a voice of thunder. Trotsky admired his enormous talent, his capacity to invent new images, and his devotion to the proletariat, while remaining unmoved by his characteristic grandiloquence. "Mayakovsky," he wrote, "describes love as though it were the migration of nations." Lenin, with a more sensitive feeling for Russian literature, found Mayakovsky virtually incomprehensible, and wondered why the government printing office was publishing his works. Surprisingly, Lenin was outvoted. Pouring out an endless stream of verses in praise of the Revolution, Mayakovsky became the poet laureate of revolutionary Russia.

Cartoons, posters, paintings, verses of every length, from two-line slogans to interminable epics, added to his increasing fame. He wrote film scenarios, and acted in films written by others. He was continually on the move, making speeches and reciting his verses to soldiers at the front and to factory workers and schoolchildren in the rear. He became an institution, and learned too late that there are few advantages in being institutionalized. The strident verses sometimes sounded like hoarse croakings, but in the very worst poems there is nearly always a tremendous image or a sudden lyrical impulse. Freshness, beauty, the gayest of improvisations can be found even in his poems celebrating industrial progress.

Above all Mayakovsky wanted to be known as a dramatic poet. In August, 1917, he had already sketched out *Mystery-Bouffe*, his twentieth-century version of a medieval morality play, in which the workers receive the rewards of the blessed and the monarchs and capitalist politicians are consigned to eternal damnation. He called it "a heroic, epic, and satiric representation of our era," but in fact it was a brilliant farce in six acts designed to reflect his anarchist vision of the world. There was nothing particularly Bolshevik about the play: the Russian Anarchists, Social Revolutionaries, and Mensheviks all agreed that the workers would inherit the earth. He worked on the play at intervals during the first year of the Revolution. It was finished in October, 1918, and immediately produced by Meyerhold, with the author designing the sets. He wrote in his diary: "Finished *Mystery-Bouffe*. Read it, much talk about it.

Acted three times, then hammered. Replaced by Macbeths." A second, somewhat longer version was produced in 1921 as an entertainment for the benefit of visiting delegates to the Congress of the Comintern.

The plot of *Mystery-Bouffe* is charmingly simple. A flood has overwhelmed the world, leaving only the North Pole above the surface of the waters. The survivors consist of seven pairs of Clean and seven pairs of Unclean. The Clean are typical representatives of the capitalist world which has been swept away in the flood. They include the Negus of Abyssinia, Clemenceau, Lloyd George (indistinguishable from an Arctic walrus), a Russian speculator, and an American with a large bank account. The Unclean are the workers of the world, now at last united in adversity. They include a miner, a lamplighter, a carpenter, a laundress. The Unclean build an Ark, but the capitalists with their usual perversity take command of it. Then The Unclean revolt and toss The Clean overboard, having observed that the Negus of Abyssinia eats all the food and the politicians issue all the commands. So The Unclean set out on their voyage to Ararat, the Promised Land, without benefit of monarchs or any commandments but their own.

Ararat is in sight, or they think it is in sight, when they are presented with an extraordinary apparition – a man walking across the waters toward them. On the stage the role of the apparition was played by Mayakovsky. "My Paradise is for everyone *except* the poor in spirit," says the mysterious stranger, as he steps on the deck. In his deafening voice he offers them the promise of the earthly kingdom:

Come unto me
all you who have calmly stabbed the enemy,
and then walked away from his corpse
with a song on your lips!

This is not blasphemy: this is merely the age-old portrait of the Christ who has no sympathy for the rich and the powerful of this world. "Heaven is within your reach," he says, "and the poor shall be under my protection and given the wealth of the earth." Then mysteriously he vanishes, and the chorus intones:

Who is he?
Who is that free spirit?
Who is he –
that nameless one?
Who is he,
with no country of his own?
Why did he come?
What prophecies did he utter?

It is a moment of extraordinary poignancy: the echoes of one mystery, written in Church Slavonic, irrupting into the mystery of the proletarian victory. Mayakovsky knew what he was doing when he played the role of the stranger coming over the sea, for he liked to keep the best verses for himself.

In the following scene we learn that The Unclean by their inexpert seamanship have blundered into Hell, a true medieval Hell inhabited by savagely laughing devils with tails, horns, and pitchforks. A few Clean have somehow survived in the hold, and the devils make short work of them. The Unclean have no difficulty breaking down the portals of Hell, advancing rapidly through Purgatory, and reaching Heaven, where Methuselah, in the company of Tolstoy, Rousseau, and St. John Chrysostom, serves as official greeter. When the saints ask what the horny-handed sons of toil are doing in Heaven, The Unclean reply: "We ourselves are Christ and Savior."

The journey through Heaven, like the journey through Hell, is the purest slapstick, and Mayakovsky has some difficulty in restraining his natural impulse for clowning. The workers steal the lightning of Jehovah, complain about the absence of heavenly chairs, wine, and the ordinary comforts of life. Why wings, when it would be more sensible to install elevators? But when they escape at last from Heaven, they are in no better plight, for they find themselves in Chaos, a country inhabited by Marxist doctrinaires. A celestial steam engine now appears and takes them to the Promised Land:

The gate flies open, and the city is revealed. What a city! The lattice-like forms of transparent factories and apartment buildings tower up toward the sky. Trains, streetcars, and automobiles stand wrapped in rainbows. In the center is a garden of stars and moons, surmounted by the radiant crown of the sun.

One might have known that the Splendid City of Mayakovsky's imagination would resemble New York's Park Avenue at Forty-eighth Street during Christmas week. Happily the vision soon fades and we are presented with a procession of Machines, Things, and Edibles. They offer bread and salt to the workers as a sign of peace, then swear eternal friendship and ask pardon for the crimes they have been forced to commit under capitalism. "All food is free," say the Edibles. "Take and eat." It is only the last of the many borrowings from the New Testament. Just as Mayakovsky imitates the verse patterns of the hymns sung in Russian churches, so he finds himself inescapably bound by Christian images and Christian concepts. He does not turn Christianity upside down; he merely tilts it, so that it can be observed freshly. In the last scene a massed chorus sings Mayakovsky's revised version of the "Internationale." It sounds, and perhaps was intended to sound, like an angelic choir.

It was a lame ending, and Mayakovsky was aware that he had not resolved his difficulties. *Mystery-Bouffe* was a failure, and rarely performed. Yet simply because it attempted the impossible feat of rewriting and rescoring a medieval mystery in terms of the proletariat's rise to power, mixing farce and folly with lyrical exaltation and wild invention, it deserves to be remembered with gratitude. He never wrote with more gusto. One does not easily forget the man walking across the waters, the clowning at the North Pole, the rape of Jehovah's lightning. Mayakovsky wore his prophetical robes when he wrote this play, for he speaks of storming the planets by airships of the commune fifty years hence. He saw electricity spreading a mantle of light across the earth, and his faith in the ultimate victory of The Unclean was unshakable. For a brief while he played the role of Aristophanes reborn in the Soviet age – and never was Aristophanes more needed.

When Mayakovsky turned to writing dramatic poetry

again, Lenin was dead, and the light had gone out of the sky. In the cruel years of Stalin he wrote with bitterness and despair. The iron bureaucracy, which Lenin brought into being and later dreaded, held all the arts in its hands. At a time when the great purges had already begun, Mayakovsky wrote his two last plays, *The Bedbug* and *The Bathhouse*, satirizing the bureaucracy and the all-powerful dictator.

III

In the eighties and nineties of the last century, there could be found in the Rumyantsev Museum in Moscow an elderly librarian with a bulbous forehead, a potato nose, and a wispy beard. He was a man of great learning and refinement, dedicated to the ascetic life, who habitually dressed shabbily and gave his money to any beggar who asked for it. His name was Nikolay Fyodorov, and he was the illegitimate son of a Circassian peasant girl by a Russian prince.

Fyodorov's subterranean influence on Russian thought was prodigious. He was the friend of Tolstoy and the philosopher Vladimir Soloviëv, who was in awe of him; Dostoyevsky admired him and rewrote long passages of *The Brothers Karamazov* after accepting his theories; and hundreds of lesser writers acknowledged him as a great thinker and a profound scholar. Fyodorov's one book, *The Common Cause*, edited from his lectures, was devoted to a statement of man's purpose in the universe, and in his eyes the purpose was nothing less than the conquest of the universe. Man will conquer the earth, command the weather, make the tides obedient to his will, and level the mountains. He will conquer the remotest stars. Above all, he will conquer death and give life to the ancestors who created him; not in new life, but in the resurrection of the dead to eternal life will he find his greatest achievement. In the eyes of Fyodorov modern technological progress demonstrated that man possessed divine powers, and those powers must be placed at the service of the dead and living alike.

In intellectual circles in Moscow and St. Petersburg Fyodorov's ideas gained wide currency. Though few people read his book, which was printed in a small limited edition, and even fewer realized that he had created a highly complex philosophical system to explain his beliefs, there was a general feeling that he must be taken seriously. On young and adventurous minds especially Fyodorov's ideas acted like a violent stimulant. Mayakovsky was introduced to them by his artist friend Vassily Chekrygin, who painted a famous series of paintings called *The Resurrection of the Dead,* and thereafter Mayakovsky made them his own, changing and adapting them to his own needs. These ideas invaded his plays.

The Bedbug, written in the fall of 1928, was a ferocious satire on communist bureaucracy. The proletarian hero Ivan Prisypkin possesses all the conventional virtues of a Soviet bureaucrat, being an ignorant vulgarian who loudly protests his loyalty to the common cause, toadies before higher officials, and insists on the proper deference being paid to his exalted station in life. He has changed his name to Pierre Skripkin, as being more euphonious and more in keeping with his new-found elegance as the wooer of Elzevira Renaissance, a manicurist and cashier in a beauty parlor. He has abandoned Zoya Berezkina, the working-class girl whom he loved until he met Elzevira, and he is entirely unmoved when she shoots herself. His future mother-in-law is delighted to have a Soviet official with impeccable credentials in the family. He has calloused hands, a Party card, a trade-union card, a vulgar manner. He is continually scratching himself, drinks prodigious quantities of vodka, and strums pleasantly on a guitar. What could be better? But the wedding feast ends abruptly when the bride's veil catches fire and all the wedding guests perish in the conflagration.

Fifty years later, when communism has been established throughout the globe, some workmen excavating on the site of the wedding feast are astonished to discover Prisypkin frozen in a block of ice in the cellar, and the Institute of Human Resurrection offers to restore him to life on condition that it receive world approval for an experiment fraught with danger to contemporary society, for who knows what diseases the corpse may have suffered? The newspaper representatives of *The Chicago Soviet News, The Madrid Milkmaid, The Shanghai Pauper, The Roman Red Gazette,* and all the other newspapers give their unqualified approval. Prisypkin's corpse is revived. So is the bedbug which accompanied him loyally in death. The Institute of Human Resurrection, having brought him to life, has no further use for him, and he is presented to the local zoo, where he inhabits a cage labeled *Philistinius vulgaris*.

From the moment he is resurrected, Prisypkin proves to be a rebel against the new communist state. He wants to play the guitar, sing romantic songs, drink, curse, and make love, but the frailties of a former age are no longer encouraged by the communist rulers. He insists on being human. For a brief moment he is permitted to step out of the cage under armed guard, and the last words are a despairing cry from the heart:

> Citizens! My people! My own people! Dear ones! How did you get here? So many of you! When did they unfreeze you? Why am I alone in the cage? Dear ones, my people! Come in with me! Why am I suffering? Citizens!

The zoo director orders the resurrected Prisypkin to be thrown back into the cage. It was all a mistake; he should never have been let out. "The noise and bright lights brought on hallucinations," he explains, and orders the band to strike up and drown the words spoken by the doomed man.

Though the play was written as a comedy, Prisypkin remains a tragic hero who derives in direct line of descent from *Vladimir Mayakovsky, A Tragedy*. Mayakovsky was perfectly aware that he was Prisypkin, or at least that there was a good deal of Prisypkin in him. He took care that the actor Ilyinsky, who played the role at the premiere in the Meyerhold State Theater in February, 1929, should look and behave as much as possible like his creator, even to adopting the same mannerisms and the same raucous voice. Mayakovsky was burlesquing Mayakovsky, and at the same time he was burlesquing the Soviet state, which had produced so many Prisypkins. Under Stalin it was necessary to pretend that the play was nothing but comic buffoonery. With Stalin dead, Soviet audiences were able to see the play performed tragically, as Mayakovsky had originally intended.

The Bedbug was a success and played for three months; the Soviet critics found little to attack in it, preferring to believe that it was a comic fantasy without relevance to anything happening at the time. They were more severe with his next play, *The Bathhouse*. This time Mayakovsky made no attempt to conceal his motives. His attacks on Soviet bureaucracy, and the aimless wanderings of the bureaucratic mind, were almost too successful, for long stretches of the play are devoted to parodies of bureaucrats at their labors, and it must be admitted that their speeches are excruciatingly boring, stupid, and distasteful. In particular the speeches of Pobedonosikov (Nose for Victory) are filled with the clichés of bureaucratic power. Pobedonosikov stands at the pinnacle of the Soviet state, for he is the chief coordinator of everything. A notice outside his office reads: "IF YOU HAVEN'T BEEN ANNOUNCED, DON'T COME IN!" Few people are announced, and the dictator spends the greater part of his time making pompous speeches in defense of his own bureaucratic methods. When The Phosphorescent Woman appears, having emerged from the year 2030 in a time machine, he engages her in a discussion of his many virtues:

> POBEDONOSIKOV: . . . I don't drink, I don't smoke, I don't give tips, I don't lean toward the Left, I don't show up late for appointments, I don't *(bending down toward her ear)* indulge in excesses, I don't spare myself on the job, I –
>
> THE PHOSPHORESCENT WOMAN: No matter what you talk about, it's always "I don't," "I don't," "I don't." Isn't there anything you "do, do, do"?
>
> POBEDONOSIKOV: "Do, do, do"? Yes, there is. I implement directives, I file resolutions, I pay my Party dues, I receive my Party maximum salary, I sign papers, I stamp them with the official seal. . . .

Pobedonosikov is very good at stamping things with his official seal, but he is altogether too lazy and too incompetent to understand that there is a world which does not want to be "officially approved." He is surrounded by sycophants and time-servers. When Chudakov (Wonder-worker) builds his time machine, which will catapult men into the future at the rate of one year per second, and invites the dictator to accompany him, his officials refuse to finance the expedition on the grounds that there exist no official directives on the subject of exploring the future. They mouth Marxist phrases, consult their card indexes, and prevent Chudakov from entering the dictator's presence. Chudakov therefore takes his machine to the dictator's private apartment, where it explodes. The Phosphorescent Woman appears, and the dictator, now properly convinced that she will lead him to the future, offers to join the expedition. Finally the machine sets out with its cargo of bureaucrats and citizens, but not before the dictator has made clear that he intends to rule over the world of the future with the same consideration for bureaucratic procedure which has characterized his rule in the past. There will be "circular letters, authorizations, copies, theses, second copies, corrections, excerpts, references, card files, resolutions, reports, minutes of proceedings, and other certifying documents" *ad infinitum*. "The moment I seize the reins of power in my new post," he declares, "I'm going to register complaints with everybody about absolutely all of you!" The prospect is not a particularly encouraging one, and as the machine hurtles forward into the unknown ages of the future, there is an explosion, and the dictator and all his officials are left sprawling on the stage, having been discarded by "the devilish wheel of time." The last words are left to Pobedonosikov, who comes to the footlights and complains bitterly to the audience. "What have you been trying to say here?" he says. "That people like me aren't of any use to communism?"

The Soviet bureaucrats who tolerated *The Bedbug* because it was largely incomprehensible found little to tolerate in *The Bathhouse*. The cutting edge was too sharp; the parodies of bureaucratic double-talk were too accurate; and the portrait of Pobedonosikov was too evidently based on the reigning dictator. Although the play was performed – for Mayakovsky had too much authority and renown to be rejected from the theater – the literary bloodhounds were in full pursuit. Mayakovsky was sternly admonished. It was hinted that he was a reactionary, a Trotskyist, or worse. Stalin, who had been keeping a watchful eye on Mayakovsky, encouraged the attacks. Vladimir Ermilov, a literary bureaucrat and hack writer who wrote innocuous studies of Dostoyevsky and Chekhov, delivered the most bitter attacks. In reply Mayakovsky hung a huge banner inside the theater with the words:

It is hard to get rid of
The swarms of bureaucrats:
Not enough bathhouses,
Not enough soap.
Bureaucrats like Ermilov
Are comforted by the critics.

Ermilov ordered that the banner be removed, and Meyerhold was reluctantly forced to yield.

Though Mayakovsky claimed to have a skin like an elephant's hide and to be impervious to criticism, he was remarkably sensitive and incapable of taking criticism gently. Enraged by the swarms of bureaucrats who now hounded him and called him to account, he protested vigorously, but the effort was too much for him. He had a nervous breakdown and entered the Kremlin Hospital for treatment; he recovered quickly and returned to his own apartment near the Lubyanka Prison. The battles with the bureaucrats had undermined his strength, and a succession of unhappy love affairs had undermined his spirit. At about ten o'clock on the morning of April 14, 1930, he placed a single bullet in his revolver and shot himself in the heart.

There were people who claimed later that he had been playing Russian roulette, but this theory was disproved by the verses and instructions he left to be read after his death. Among the papers found on his table there was a curiously jaunty verse:

"The incident is closed."
The love boat has been
Smashed against conventions.
I don't owe life anything,
And nothing will be gained
By counting over
Mutual hurts and slights.

There was another note, which read: "Tell Ermilov that it is too bad he removed the banner. We should have fought it out."

Yet Mayakovsky knew there could be no fighting against Ermilov. He died because he could no longer breathe the polluted air of Russian bureaucracy, and because the Soviet system could no longer tolerate his genius. The Ermilovs always fare better under a communist dictatorship, and in fact Vladimir Ermilov continued to occupy a position of bureaucratic importance for the rest of his long life. He died in 1965, having outlived Mayakovsky by thirty-five years.

At the height of the purges, in 1935, Stalin issued a decree commanding that special reverence be paid to the memory of Mayakovsky. "Mayakovsky was and remains the best and most talented poet of our Soviet era," he proclaimed. "Indifference to his memory and his work is a crime." The official cult of Mayakovsky was thus introduced under the highest authority. Schoolchildren all over Russia were forced to read his verses and learn them by heart. The state publishing houses produced innumerable editions of his works and interminable volumes of commentary, showing that he was a good Bolshevik who always held Stalin in high honor. Posthumous honors were showered on him: a subway station and a great square in Moscow were named after him, and statues were erected wherever there could be found an excuse for them. Of the official cult of Mayakovsky, Pasternak said: "He began to be introduced forcibly, like potatoes under Catherine the Great. This was his second death. He had no hand in it."

For the Soviet authorities the official cult was not an unmixed blessing. The government claimed him, but could not take possession of him. The legend he had created for himself was more powerful than the official caricature presented to the public, and by making his works so easily available the government defeated its own purposes. He was presented as the epitome of Soviet courage and daring, and it was forgotten that he had never joined the Communist Party and had fought relentlessly against Soviet bureaucracy. The poet who wrote *The Bedbug* and *The Bathhouse* showed with amazing clarity that he despaired of the Soviet system, its artificialities, its remoteness from life, and its terrible dogmas. As his legend grew, he became more powerful, more heretical, and more dangerous to the Soviet state, which had embraced him and could not let him go. The Soviet officials realized too late that they had canonized a heretic.

For heretic he was — to the very end, to the last breath. He never sacrificed his individuality, never submitted to the iron rules of the communist state. On the contrary, he made use of the communists for his own ends. Proud and insolent, profoundly in love with freedom, hating all bondage, he became a prophet proclaiming a new age of freedom; and he loved freedom so much that he was prepared to die for it. In this sense he was one of the authentic heroes of his time.

— ROBERT PAYNE

VLADIMIR MAYAKOVSKY

A Tragedy

Characters

VLADIMIR MAYAKOVSKY, a poet (twenty to twenty-five years old)

THE ENORMOUS WOMAN, his lady friend (fifteen to twenty feet tall; she does not speak)

OLD MAN WITH SCRAWNY BLACK CATS (several thousand years old)

MAN WITH ONE EYE AND ONE LEG

MAN WITH ONE EAR

[MAN WITH ONE ARM]

MAN WITHOUT A HEAD

MAN WITH A LONG DRAWN-OUT FACE

MAN WITH TWO KISSES

CONVENTIONAL YOUNG MAN

WOMAN WITH A TINY TEAR

WOMAN WITH A TEAR

WOMAN WITH A GREAT BIG TEAR

NEWSBOYS, [CHILD KISSES], etc.

[OLD MAN WITH ONE SHORN CAT]

Prologue

(spoken by MAYAKOVSKY*)*

Can you understand
why I,
quite calmly,
through a hailstorm of jeers,
carry my soul on a platter
to be dined on by future years?
On the unshaven cheek of the plazas,
trickling down like a useless tear,
I
may well be
the last poet there is.
Have you noticed,
dangling
above the pebbled paths,
the striped face of boredom – hanged?
And on lathery necks
of rushing rivers,
bridges wringing their iron hands?
The sky is weeping –
uncontrollably,
loudly;
a cloud,
its little mouth twisted, is looking wry,
like a woman expecting a baby,
to whom God has tossed an idiot blind in one eye.
With swollen fingers sprouting reddish hairs,
the sun has caressed you with a gadfly's persistence:
in your souls, a slave has been kissed to death.
I, undaunted,
have borne my hatred for sunlight through centuries,
my soul stretched taut as the nerves of a wire.

I
am king of lights!
Come to me,
you who ripped the silence,
you who howled
because the nooses of noon were too tight!
I will reveal to you,
with words
as simple as bellowing,
our new souls –
humming
like the arcs of street lights.
I shall merely touch your heads with my fingers,
and you
will grow lips
for enormous kisses,
and tongues
native to all peoples.
Then I, my shabby soul hobbling,
shall go off to my throne
with the starry holes in the worn-out dome.
I'll lie down,
radiant,
clothed in laziness,
on a soft couch of genuine *dreck;*
and quietly,
kissing the knees of the crossties,
the wheel of a locomotive will embrace my neck.

ACT I

Jolly. The stage represents a city with its spider web of streets. A beggars' holiday. MAYAKOVSKY *alone. Passersby bring him food: the iron herring from a street sign; a huge golden twisted loaf of bread; swatches of yellow velvet.*

MAYAKOVSKY

Ladies and gentlemen!
Patch up my soul
so the emptiness can't leak out!
I don't know whether a gob of spit is an insult or not!
I'm dry as a stone image.
They've milked me like a cow.
Ladies and gentlemen!
If you wish,
a remarkable poet will dance for you right here and now.
(Enter the OLD MAN WITH SCRAWNY BLACK CATS. *He strokes them. He is all beard.)*
Seek out the fat ones in their shell-like dwellings,
and beat out revels on the drum of the belly!
Catch the stupid and deaf by the feet,
and blow in their ears like the nostrils of a flute.
Break open the bottoms of barrels of fury,
for I eat the hot cobblestones of thought.
Today, as you toast me with raucous shouts,
I shall crown myself with my folly.
(The stage gradually fills with people: the MAN WITH ONE EAR, *the* MAN WITHOUT A HEAD, et al. *They are torpid. Confusion sets in. They continue to eat.)*
A barefooted jeweler cutting faceted verses,

fluffing up featherbeds in the homes of others,
today I shall light up a worldwide fair
for all such wealthy and motley beggars!

OLD MAN WITH SCRAWNY BLACK CATS

Stop it!
You shake babies' rattles to entertain sages. Why?
I'm old – a thousand-year-old gaffer.
And I see that in you an anguished cry
has been crucified on a cross of laughter.
A gigantic grief lay over the town –
and hundreds of tiny griefs.
But the candles and lights, with their hubbub of quarreling,
drowned out the whispers of dawns.
Soft moons have no power over us: the blaze
of lights is more stylish, and harsher;
in the land of cities, having dubbed themselves masters,
soulless Things want to put an end to our days.
From the heavens, a God gone mad
looks down on the howling human horde,
his hands in his tattered beard,
eaten thin by the dust of roads.
He's God,
yet He warns of a cruel retribution;
but the midriff in your poor, shabby souls is worn thin.
Get rid of Him!
Go stroke cats –
stroke cats that are black and scrawny!
You will grasp huge bellies boastfully;
you will puff out sleek, cream-puff cheeks.
Only in cats
whose fur is shot through with blackness
will you catch flashes of electric eyes.
The entire catch of those flashes
(a big catch!)
we'll pour into wires –
those muscles of traction:
streetcars will start off in a rush;
the flame of wicks
will glow in the night like triumphant banners.

The world, in gay greasepaint, will stir into action;
the flowers in the windows will strut, peacock bright;
people will travel on rails –
always trailed
by cats, more cats, lots of black cats!
We'll pin the sun on the gowns of our sweethearts;
we'll adorn them with glittering brooches of stars.
Leave your apartments!
Go stroke cats –
stroke cats that are black and scrawny!

MAN WITH ONE EAR

That's the truth!
Above the city,
in the realm of the weathervanes
a woman –
dark caverns of eyelids –
rushes around
throwing gobs of spit down on the sidewalk;
and the gobs grow into huge invalids.
Above the city, someone paid for a crime:
people crowded together
and ran in a herd.
And there,
on the wallpaper,
among the shadows of wine,
a wrinkled little old man wept over a grand piano.
(The others crowd around him.)
Above the city the legend of torments spreads wide.
Catch hold of a note,
and your fingers will bleed!
The musician can't tear his hands free
from the furious keyboard's white teeth!
(All are alarmed.)
And now
today,
since morning,
a Spanish dance has been chiseling out lips
in my soul.
I was walking along, twitching, my hands spread out
wide,

and on every side
smokestacks were dancing on rooftops,
and their knees made a shape like 44.
Sirs!
Just consider!
Is this really right?
Even the side streets rolled up their sleeves for a fight.
And my own sorrow grows —
alarming and unaccountable —
like a tear on a weeping dog's nose.
(The sense of alarm increases.)

OLD MAN WITH SCRAWNY BLACK CATS
See what I mean?
Things must be destroyed!
I was right when I sensed the foe in their endearments;

MAN WITH A LONG DRAWN-OUT FACE
But maybe Things should be loved.
Perhaps Things have different souls from ours.

MAN WITH ONE ARM
A good many Things are sewed inside out.
Their hearts know no anger;
They're deaf to wrath.

MAN WITH A LONG DRAWN-OUT FACE *(joyously agreeing)*
And in the place where a man's mouth is carved out,
many Things have an ear attached!

MAYAKOVSKY *(raises one hand, advances to center)*
Don't smear the ends of hearts with your anger!
I,
my children,
will teach you most strictly and by the rod.
All you people here
are mere
bells on the duncecap of God.
I,
with a foot swollen from searching,
have walked all through
your country
and several other lands, too,
in the cloak and mask of darkness.
I was searching

for her,
the soul no one had seen,
in order to put her healing flowers
into the wounds of my lips.

(A pause)

And again,
like a slave
in a bloody sweat,
I rock my body with madness.
By the way
I did find her once –
that soul.
She came out
in a blue dressing gown,
and said:
"Sit down.
I've been waiting a long time for you.
Wouldn't you like a glass of tea?"

(A pause)

I'm a poet.
I've wiped out the differences
between faces like mine and those of strangers.
I have sought out my sisters in the pus of morgues.
I have kissed the sick most exquisitely.
But today,
on a bonfire's yellow flames,
hiding more deeply the tears of the seas,
I'll throw both the sisters' shame
and the wrinkles of gray-haired mothers.
On plates from fancy salons,
we'll chomp at you, meat, for centuries!

(THE ENORMOUS WOMAN *is unveiled. Fear. The* CONVENTIONAL YOUNG MAN *rushes in. A hubbub.)*

(Aside, quietly)

Ladies and gentlemen!
They tell me
that somewhere –
in Brazil, most probably –
there is one really happy man!

CONVENTIONAL YOUNG MAN *(runs up to each of the others in turn, kissing them)*

Ladies and gentlemen!
Wait!
Ladies and gentlemen!
Sir,
sir,
tell me quickly: Do you
and the others
want to burn *mothers?*
Gentlemen!
The mind of man is keen,
but before the world's mysteries it quails.
Yet you're going to start a blaze
with the treasures of knowledge and books!
I've thought up a machine for slicing ham.
I'm really quite clever, if you please!
I know a man
who's been working for twenty-five years
on a trap for catching fleas.
I have a wife
who'll soon give birth to a son or a daughter.
Yet you talk of monstrous evils!
Intelligent people!
Why, it's almost uncivil!

MAN WITH ONE EAR

Young man,
get up on a soapbox!

VOICE FROM THE CROWD

A barrel would be better!

MAN WITH ONE EAR

If you don't, we can't see you!

CONVENTIONAL YOUNG MAN

There's nothing to laugh at!
I have a brother –
a little one.
You'll come and chomp on his bones.
You want to eat up everything!

(Alarm. Sirens. Offstage, cries of "Britches! Britches!")

MAYAKOVSKY

Lay off it!
(The CONVENTIONAL YOUNG MAN *is surrounded.)*
If you'd gone without food as I've gone without food,
you
would chew
on the distant expanses of West and East,
as the smoke-blackened mugs of factories feast
on the bone of the heavens!

CONVENTIONAL YOUNG MAN

What?
You mean love is no good?
I have a sister – Sonya is her name.
(On his knees)
Kind people,
please don't start to spill blood!
Dear ones,
let's not have any flames!
(Heightened sense of alarm. Shots. A sewer pipe begins slowly to draw out one long note. The iron of the roof starts to wail.)

MAN WITH A LONG DRAWN-OUT FACE

If you had loved as I have loved,
you would murder love;
or else, on a scaffold reared high,
you'd debauch
the shaggy, sweat-dripping sky
and the milky-innocent stars.

MAN WITH ONE EAR

Your women don't know
how to love: they are swollen like sponges from kisses.
(Blows from hundreds of feet strike the taut belly of the city square.)

MAN WITH A LONG DRAWN-OUT FACE

And from my soul you can sew,
also,
such elegant dresses!
(The excitement is uncontrollable. Everyone crowds around THE ENORMOUS WOMAN. *They hoist*

her up on their shoulders and start to carry her off.)

ALL

We are going to where
a prophet, because of his sanctity,
was crucified; there,
we'll yield up our bodies to a naked dance;
and on the black granite of sin and vice,
we'll raise a monument to red meat.

(They carry THE ENORMOUS WOMAN *to the door. Enter the* MAN WITH ONE EYE AND ONE LEG. *He is joyous. The madness breaks all bonds. They drop* THE ENORMOUS WOMAN.)

MAN WITH ONE EYE AND ONE LEG

Stop!
On the street –
where everyone wears,
like a burden,
the same face –
Old Lady Time just now gave birth
to a huge
revolt wearing a grimace!
What a laugh!
Old-timers went numb when they saw the snouts
of the years that came crawling out;
on the foreheads of cities
anger swelled up into rivers
of thousand-mile-long veins.
Slowly,
in terror,
arrows of hair
rose up on the bald pate of Time.
Suddenly,
all things went rushing off, ripping
their voices,
and casting off tatters of outworn names.
Wineshop windows, all on their own,
splashed in the bottoms of bottles,
as though stirred by the finger of Satan.
From the shop of a tailor who'd fainted,

trousers escaped
and went walking along –
alone,
without human buttocks!
Out of a bedroom,
a drunken commode –
its black maw agape –
came stumbling.
Corsets wept, afraid of tumbling
down from signs reading "ROBES ET MODES."
Every galosh was stern and straitlaced.
Stockings, like sluts,
winked flirty eyes.
I flew along like a violent curse.
My other leg is still trying to catch up –
it's a block behind.
What do you mean,
you people,
proclaiming that I'm a cripple?
You old,
fat,
paunchy
enemies?
Today,
in the whole world, you won't find
one person
with two
identical knees!

CURTAIN

ACT II

Depressing. A plaza in a new city. MAYAKOVSKY *is now wearing a toga and laurel wreath. Behind the door, many feet.*

MAN WITH ONE EYE AND ONE LEG *(deferentially)*

Poet!
Poet!
They've made you a prince!
Your vassals
are outside the door, crowding around,
sucking their thumbs.
Before each one of them, on the ground,
is some kind of ridiculous vessel.

MAYAKOVSKY

Well, I don't care,
let them come in.

(WOMEN WITH BUNDLES, *timidly. Many of them bow.)*

WOMAN WITH A TINY TEAR

Here's my tear –
take it!
It's no use to me.
Here.
That's all right.
It's white –
silk made of filaments
from eyes transmitting grief.

MAYAKOVSKY *(uneasy)*

I don't need it.
Why give it to me?

(To the next woman)

Are your eyes swollen, too?

WOMAN WITH A TEAR *(unconcerned)*

What's that to you?
My son is dying.
No trouble.
Here's another tear.
You could put it on your shoe –
it would make a fine buckle.

*(*MAYAKOVSKY *is frightened.)*

WOMAN WITH A GREAT BIG TEAR

Just pretend you don't see
that I'm
covered with grime.
I'll wash up –
I'll get clean as can be.
Here's one more tear for you –
a great big one this time,
with nothing to do.

MAYAKOVSKY

That's enough!
I have heaps of them now.
And besides, I must go.
Who's that charming brunette?

NEWSBOYS

Figaro!
Figaro!
Gazette!

(The MAN WITH TWO KISSES *enters. All look around and talk at once.)*

ALL

Look at him!
What a savage!
Step back a bit!
It's dark!
Let him in!
Young man,
don't hiccup.

MAN WITHOUT A HEAD

Eee-ee-ee-ee.
Eh-eh-eh-eh.

MAN WITH TWO KISSES

The clouds are surrenderring to the sky –
they're vile and flabby.
The day is done.
The girls of the air are also grabby
for gold: they only want money.

MAYAKOVSKY

What's that?

MAN WITH TWO KISSES

They only want money – and money alone!

VOICES

Not so loud!
Not so loud!

MAN WITH TWO KISSES *(does a dance with balls full of holes)*

A man who was big and all dirty
received two kisses as a gift.
He was an awkward fellow
and didn't know
what to do with them –
where they should go.
The whole town,
bedecked for the holiday,
was singing hallelujahs in the cathedrals,
and people were out in their Sunday best.
But the man was cold;
there were oval-shaped holes in the soles
of his shoes. He chose one of the kisses –
bigger than the other –
and put it on like his galoshes.
But the weather
was bitter cold, and nipped at his fingers.
"Oh, bother!"
said the angry man.
"I'll throw these useless kisses away!"
And he did.
But suddenly,
one of the kisses grew ears;
it toddled about;
and then in a thin, squeaky voice, cried out:
"Mama!"

And the man was afraid.
He wrapped up the shivering
little body
in the rags of his soul,
and took it home
to put it into a light-blue picture frame.
For a long time he rummaged in dusty trunks,
trying to find the frame.
When he looked around,
the kiss was lying there on a sofa:
huge,
fat,
tall –
first laughing,
then in a rage.
"Good Lord!"
the man said, beginning to cry.
"I never believed I'd get so tired!
I'll just have to hang myself, that's all!"
While he dangled there –
vile,
pitiful –
in their bedrooms, women
(factories without smoke or smokestacks)
manufactured kisses by the millions –
all kinds,
both big
and little –
with the meaty levers of lips that smack.

CHILD KISSES *(entering; playfully)*
They've turned out a lot of us!
Take these!
Any minute the others will come.
So far, there's just eight.
I'm
Mitya.
Please!

(Each one puts down a tear.)

MAYAKOVSKY
Gentlemen!

Listen!
I can't stand it!
It's all right for you.
But what about me, with my pain?

THREATENING VOICES

You just go on talking that way,
and we'll make you into a stew –
like a rabbit!

OLD MAN WITH ONE SHORN CAT

You're the only one who can sing songs.
(Points to the pile of tears.)
Take them away to your pretty God!

MAYAKOVSKY

Let me sit down!
(They don't allow it. MAYAKOVSKY *hesitates awkwardly, then gathers the tears into his suitcase. He stands there, holding the suitcase.)*
All right!
Make way for me, then!
I thought
I'd be joyful:
with eyes clear and bright,
I would sit on the throne
like a pampered Greek.
But no!
Never,
dear roads,
will I forget
your thin legs
and the gray hairs of the northern rivers.
And so today
I'll go out through the city,
leaving
shred after shred of my tattered soul
on the spears of houses.
And the moon will go with me
to where
the dome of the sky is ripped out.
She'll come up beside me,
and briefly try on my derby hat.

I,
with my heavy load,
will walk on;
I'll stumble and fall;
I'll crawl
further
northward,
to where,
in the vise of infinite anguish,
the fanatic sea
with the fingers of waves
tears at its breast
eternally.
I'll drag myself there
exhausted;
and in my last ravings
I'll throw your tears
to the dark god of storms,
at the source of bestial faiths.

CURTAIN

Epilogue

(*spoken by* MAYAKOVSKY)

I wrote all this
about you —
poor drudges!
It's too bad I had no bosom: I'd have fed
all of you, like a sweet little old nanny.
But right now I'm a bit dried up —
and a little bit touched in the head.
On the other hand,
who'd
have given his thoughts such inhuman latitude?
Who, and where?
It was I
who stuck my finger into the sky:[1]
I proved that He's
a thief!
Sometimes it seems to me
that I'm a Dutch rooster,
or else
a Pskovian king.
But at other times, what pleases me
more than anything
is my own name:
Vladimir Mayakovsky.

CURTAIN

1913

MYSTERY-BOUFFE

A Heroic, Epic, and Satiric Representation of Our Era

(Second Version 1921)

Mystery-Bouffe is a high road — the high road of the Revolution. No one can predict with certainty how many more mountains will have to be blasted away by those of us who are traveling that high road. Today the name of Lloyd George rings harshly in our ears; but tomorrow he will have been forgotten even by the English. Today the will of millions is surging toward the Commune; in another fifty years the airborne battleships of the Commune may be rushing to the attack of distant planets.

Therefore, though I have kept to the high road (the form) [in this second version of *Mystery-Bouffe*], I have in part changed the landscape (the content).

In the future, all persons performing, presenting, reading, or publishing *Mystery-Bouffe* should change the content, making it contemporary, immediate, up-to-the-minute.

THE CLEAN

THE UNCLEAN

Characters[1]

1. SEVEN PAIRS OF THE CLEAN
   1. THE NEGUS of ABYSSINIA
   2. AN INDIAN RAJA
   3. A TURKISH PASHA
   4. A RUSSIAN MERCHANT (SPECULATOR)
   5. A CHINESE
   6. A WELL-FED PERSIAN
   7. CLEMENCEAU
   8. A GERMAN
   9. A RUSSIAN PRIEST
   10. AN AUSTRALIAN
   11. HIS WIFE
   12. LLOYD GEORGE
   13. AN AMERICAN
   14. A DIPLOMAT

2. SEVEN PAIRS OF THE UNCLEAN
   1. A SOLDIER OF THE RED ARMY
   2. A LAMPLIGHTER
   3. A TRUCK DRIVER
   4. A MINER
   5. A CARPENTER
   6. A FARMHAND
   7. A SERVANT (FEMALE)
   8. A BLACKSMITH
   9. A BAKER
   10. A LAUNDRESS
   11. A SEAMSTRESS
   12. A LOCOMOTIVE ENGINEER
   13. AN ESKIMO FISHERMAN
   14. AN ESKIMO HUNTER

3. A COMPROMISER[2]

4. AN INTELLECTUAL

5. THE LADY WITH THE HATBOXES

6. DEVILS
   1. BEELZEBUB
   2. MASTER-OF-CEREMONIES DEVIL
   3. FIRST MESSENGER
   4. SECOND MESSENGER
   5. GUARD
   6. TWENTY OF THE CLEAN WITH HORNS AND TAILS

(CHARACTERS CONT.)

7. SAINTS
   1. METHUSELAH
   2. JEAN-JACQUES ROUSSEAU
   3. LEO TOLSTOY
   4. GABRIEL
   5. FIRST ANGEL
   6. SECOND ANGEL
   7. ANGELS

8. JEHOVAH

9. ACTORS OF THE PROMISED LAND
   1. A HAMMER
   2. A SICKLE
   3. MACHINES
   4. TRAINS
   5. AUTOMOBILES
   6. A CARPENTER'S PLANE
   7. TONGS
   8. A NEEDLE
   9. A SAW
   10. BREAD
   11. SALT
   12. SUGAR
   13. FABRICS
   14. A BOOT
   15. A BOARD AND LEVER

10. THE MAN OF THE FUTURE

Settings of the Acts

I – The entire universe.
II – The Ark.
III – Hell.
IV – Paradise.
V – Land of Chaos.
VI – The Promised Land.

Prologue

(*Spoken by one of* THE UNCLEAN)

In just a minute
we'll present to your view
our *Mystery-Bouffe.*
But first I must say a few words.
This play
is something new.
Without help, nobody has yet succeeded
in jumping higher than his head.
Likewise, a new play must be preceded
by a prologue, or else it's dead.
First, let me ask you:
Why is this playhouse in such a mess?
To right-thinking people
it's a scandal, no less!
But then what makes you go to see a show?
You do it for pleasure –
isn't that so?
But is the pleasure really so great, after all,
if you're looking just at the stage?
The stage, you know,
is only one-third of the hall.
Therefore,
at an interesting show,
if things are set up properly,
your pleasure is multiplied by three.[1]
But if the play isn't interesting,
then you're wasting your time
looking at even one-third of what's happening.
For other theatrical companies
the spectacle doesn't matter:
for them

the stage
is a keyhole without a key.
"Just sit there quietly," they say to you,
"either straight or sidewise,
and look at a slice of other folks' lives."
You look – and what do you see?
Uncle Vanya
and Auntie Manya
parked on a sofa as they chatter.
But we don't care
about uncles or aunts:
you can find them at home – or anywhere!
We, too, will show you life that's real –
very!
But life transformed by the theater into a spectacle most extraordinary!

The gist of Act One is as follows:
the world is leaking.
Then comes a stampede:
everyone flees Revolution's flood.
There are seven pairs of The Unclean,
and seven pairs of The Clean
(that is, fourteen poor proletarians
and fourteen important bourgeois),
and in between,
with a pair of tear-stained cheeks,
a miserable little Menshevik.
The North Pole is flooded,
the last refuge is gone.
So they all begin building,
not just an Ark,
but a great big super-duper one.

In Act Two the public
takes a trip on the ark:
here you'll find both autocracy
and a democratic republic.
Finally,

while the Menshevik howls,
The Clean are thrown overboard head over heels.

In the Third Act we show and tell
how the workers
have nothing to be afraid of –
not even the devils in Hell.
In Act Four –
laugh till it brings tears to your eyes! –
we show the bowers of Paradise.

In Act Five, Devastation or Chaos,
opening wide her huge yap,
destroys things and gobbles them up.
But we, though we worked in semistarvation,
succeeded
in conquering Devastation.

In the Sixth Act
comes the Commune.
Everyone
must sing out at the top of his voice!

Look as hard as you can!
Is everything ready –
both up in Heaven
and Down Below?
(VOICE FROM OFFSTAGE: Rea-dy!)
On with the show!

ACT I

In the glow of the Northern Lights, the terrestrial globe, its South Pole resting on a floor of ice. The entire globe is covered with rope ladders representing the parallels and meridians. Between two walruses supporting the world stands an ESKIMO HUNTER *with his finger stuck into the Earth. He is shouting at an* ESKIMO FISHERMAN *reclining in front of a campfire.*

HUNTER

Oh! Oh! Oh!

FISHERMAN

Just listen to that hollering!
He's got nothing better to do
than stick his finger into the world.

HUNTER

A hole!

FISHERMAN

Where?

HUNTER

It's leaking.

FISHERMAN

What's leaking?

HUNTER

The world!

FISHERMAN *(jumps up, runs over to the* HUNTER, *and looks under his finger)*

O-o-o-oh!
The work of unclean hands!
Damn!
I'll go and notify the Arctic Circle.

(He starts to run off but encounters a GERMAN,

who jumps out at him from behind the edge of the world, wringing out his wet coat sleeves. The GERMAN *tries to buttonhole the* ESKIMO FISHERMAN, *but finding no buttons on the latter's parka, clutches the fur.)*

GERMAN

Herr Eskimo!
Herr Eskimo!
Something most urgent!
Wait just a moment. . . .

FISHERMAN

Well, what is it?

GERMAN

Let me explain.
Today I was sitting in a restaurant
on the Friedrichstrasse.
Through the window the sunlight
was so enticing!
The day,
like a bourgeois before the Revolution,
was serene.
People were sitting there
quietly Scheidemannizing.[1]
When I'd finished my soup,
I looked at the Eiffel towers of bottles on the shelf,
and I asked myself:
What kind of beef shall I have today?
Or should I have beef at all?
I looked again,
and my food stuck in my throat:
something was wrong out there in the street!
The statues of the Hohenzollerns,
which had been standing there among the camomiles,
suddenly flew upward, head over heels!
Then came a roar.
I rushed up to the roof.
A waterless flood
was surging around the building,
drowning out all other sounds;
it swept on,

engulfing whole districts of the city.
Berlin was an angry sea, raving
in bass notes of invisible waves.
To,
and fro,
above,
below,
went houses like men-of-war.
And before I even had time to wonder
whether this was the doing of Foch, or —

FISHERMAN

Cut it short!

GERMAN

I was soaked to the skin.
I looked around me:
everything was dry,
yet it poured, and poured, and poured.
Suddenly
a picture more awesome than Pompeii's destruction
unfolded before me:
Berlin was torn up by the roots
and smelted
in the abyss — the blast furnace of the world.
I found myself on the crest
of villages that had melted.
I summoned up all my Yacht Club know-how;
and here before you,
dearest sir,
is all that remains of Europe now.

FISHERMAN

N-n-not much.

GERMAN

Naturally, things will calm down
in a day or two.

FISHERMAN

Why all this beating about the bush?
What do you want? This is no place for you.

GERMAN *(pointing in a horizontal direction)*

Allow me to rest beside your most honorable seals.

(The FISHERMAN, *annoyed, jerks his thumb to-*

ward the campfire and goes off in the opposite direction, but bumps into a pair of dripping wet AUSTRALIANS, *who have come running out from behind the other edge of the world.)*

FISHERMAN *(taking a step backward in astonishment)*

When you see faces like that, words fail yuh!

AUSTRALIAN AND HIS WIFE *(together)*

We're from Australia.

AUSTRALIAN

I'm an Australian.
We had everything.
For instance:
a palm tree, a cactus, a dingo, a platypus.

AUSTRALIAN'S WIFE *(weeping with an onrush of emotion)*

And now it's all up with us!
We had to let everything go.
All is lost: the dingo,
the platypus, the cactus, the palm tree –
they've sunk down in the sea;
they're all at the bottom. . . .

FISHERMAN *(pointing to the* GERMAN, *who has stretched himself out beside the walruses)*

Better go join him –
keep him company.

(He once more starts to leave, but stops when he hears two voices from the other side of the world.)

FIRST VOICE

Oo-hoo there, Derby!

SECOND VOICE

Ooh-hoo there, Top-hat!

FIRST VOICE

It's getting worse!
Hang on to the northern parallel!

SECOND VOICE

It's getting rough!
Grab hold of the southern meridian!

*(*LLOYD GEORGE *and* CLEMENCEAU *clamber down the ropes of the earth's parallels and meridians. Each one plants his own national flag.)*

LLOYD GEORGE

My flag is planted.
I'm undisputed master in this snowy clime.

CLEMENCEAU

I beg to differ!
My flag was set up first.
This colony is mine.

LLOYD GEORGE *(laying out some trading goods)*

No, it's not. It's mine.
I'm already trading, see?

CLEMENCEAU *(getting angry)*

Oh, no! It belongs to me.
Go look for another place.

LLOYD GEORGE *(furious)*

What?
You can go to hell!

CLEMENCEAU

What?
Why, I'll smash your face!

LLOYD GEORGE *(goes for* CLEMENCEAU *with clenched fists)*

Britannia, hip, hip!

CLEMENCEAU *(goes for* LLOYD GEORGE *with clenched fists)*

Vive la France!

AUSTRALIAN *(rushing up to separate them)*

A fine lot, I must say!
No better than a bunch of thugs.
There are no more empires left today,
or imperial gold coins, either.
Yet still they punch each other's mugs!

FISHERMAN

Oh, bother –
you imperialists!

GERMAN

Stop it, now! Cut it out!

FISHERMAN

How they can shout!
(He is again making ready to leave, when a RUSSIAN MERCHANT *drops down, landing right on the* FISHERMAN'S *head.)*

MERCHANT

Honorable sirs,
I am extremely annoyed!
If I were Asian,
this wouldn't be so amazing,
because
the Celestial Soviet has decreed: "Asia must be destroyed."
But Asiatic is one thing I never was.
(He calms down a little.)
Back in Tula yesterday,
as I sat peacefully at home,
my door was pushed in from outside.
Well, thought I,
that's the secret police.
Needless to say,
I felt weak in the knees.
But God is most gracious and kind:
it wasn't the Cheka,[2] but the wind.
There came a slight drizzle,
then it started to pour:
more, and still more;
the water rose higher;
streets were flowing,
roofs went flying. . . .

ALL

Quiet! Quiet!

CLEMENCEAU

Do you hear what I hear?
The tramping of feet coming near?

VOICES FROM AN APPROACHING MULTITUDE

The flood! By the flood! To the flood! About
the flood! Of the flood!

LLOYD GEORGE *(terrified)*

Lord help us!
Misfortune flows as from a water main:
here comes that Eastern Question once again!

(Enter the NEGUS OF ABYSSINIA, *followed by a* CHINESE, *a* PERSIAN, *a* TURKISH PASHA, *a* RAJA, *a* RUSSIAN PRIEST, *a* COMPROMISER, *a* DIPLOMAT, *and*

an INTELLECTUAL.[3] *Bringing up the rear of the procession are all seven pairs of* THE UNCLEAN, *who have come together from all directions.)*

NEGUS

I'm slightly blacker than the snow –
that is quite true.
Still, I'm the Negus of Abyssinia:
My respects to you.
I just now came from Africa, a land
through which the Nile, that boa-constrictor river,
used to wend its way.
But the Nile got out of hand:
it swallowed up my kingdom, and the rest of Africa, too.
I've lost my holdings – that is quite true –
But nevertheless . . .

FISHERMAN *(annoyed)*

"That is quite true. . . .
Still, my respects to you."
We've heard all that before!

NEGUS

I must ask you not to forget
you are speaking to the Negus;
and the Negus wants something to eat.
What's that? A dog?
Looks like a tasty bit of meat.

FISHERMAN

Dog, my ass!
That's a walrus.

(The NEGUS *tries to sit down on* LLOYD GEORGE, *who looks exactly like a walrus.)*

Go on and sit down, but don't splash ink on anybody.

LLOYD GEORGE *(in alarm)*

I'm not a walrus! Don't use me for a chair!
That's a walrus over there.
I'm not a walrus – not me!
I'm Lloyd George, as you can see.

FISHERMAN *(to the others in the procession)*

What do you want?

CHINESE

Nothing!
Nothing!
China, my homeland, has been engulfed!

PERSIAN

Persia,
dear Persia, has sunk to the bottom of the sea!

RAJA

Even India,
celestial India, is gone!

PASHA

And all that's left of Turkey is a memory!

(From the throng of THE UNCLEAN *a* LADY *breaks through; she is carrying an infinite number of hatboxes.)*

LADY

Careful, there!
That silk might tear –
it's very fine.

(To the FISHERMAN*)*

My good man,
help me set down these boxes.

A VOICE FROM THE GROUP OF THE CLEAN

What a darling!
She whets my appetite!

FISHERMAN

She's nothing but a parasite!

CLEMENCEAU

And what is your nationality?

LADY

My citizenship is most various.
At first I was Russian;
but in Russia I felt confined.
Those Bolsheviks are so nefarious!
I'm an elegant woman, with a soul that is very refined.
So I became an Estonian.
But the Bolsheviks came up to the border,
so I became a Ukrainian.
In short order,
they captured Kharkov ten times or more;

but I'd gone to Odessa on the Black Sea shore.
They seized Odessa; but the White regiments
still held the Crimea, so that's where I went.
The Whites were chased across land and sea,
but by then I was a Turkish lady,
strolling the streets of Istanbul.
The Bolsheviks drew near again,
but I was already a Parisienne,
strolling the streets of the French capital.
I've changed countries forty times or more.
Now I'm a Kamchatkan citizeness.
But Arctic summers are such a bore –
no chance to show off a new dress!

FISHERMAN *(shouting at* THE CLEAN*)*

Quiet! Quiet!
What is that howling?

COMPROMISER *(in hysterics, extricating himself from the crowd)*

Please listen to me!
I've had all I can bear!
Listen, please!
What's going on here?
There's not a dry spot left on earth!
Leave me in peace!
I want to go home
to my own study, and lock the door.
Listen!
I just can't take any more!
I thought the flood would be a nice moderate one, according to Kautsky,[4]
with the wolves well-fed
and the lambs untouched.
But now
people are killing each other dead!
Dear Whites!
Dear Reds!
Listen to me! This is just too much![5]

CLEMENCEAU

Oh, stop rubbing your eyes
and biting your lip!

(To THE UNCLEAN, *who are approaching the campfire; in a haughty tone of voice)*

And you – what are your nationalities?

THE UNCLEAN *(together)*

We're a roving band,
used to wandering through the world.
We have no nationality:
labor is our native land.

CLEMENCEAU

Old arias!

THE CLEAN *(in frightened voices)*

They're proletarians!
Proletarians!
Proletarians!

BLACKSMITH *(to* CLEMENCEAU, *slapping him on his sizable belly)*

The roar of the flood makes your ears ring, eh?

LAUNDRESS *(also to* CLEMENCEAU, *in a shrill, mocking voice)*

So you'd like to lie down for a nice snooze in bed?
Go to the mines or the trenches instead!

SOLDIER OF THE RED ARMY *(menacingly)*

The trenches would be better –
they're a lot wetter.

(Seeing a "conflict" in the making between THE CLEAN *and* THE UNCLEAN, *the* COMPROMISER *rushes in to separate them.)*

COMPROMISER

Dear friends! Stop it, please! Don't cause trouble!
Stop glaring at each other like that!
Shake hands –
embrace one another.
Gentlemen, comrades,
we must somehow agree. . . .

CLEMENCEAU *(wrathfully)*

Agree with *them?*
That's too much for me!

(Both the FISHERMAN *and* CLEMENCEAU *belabor the* COMPROMISER *with blows on the neck.)*

FISHERMAN

Oh, you compromiser!

You puny little compromiser, you!

COMPROMISER *(in a whining voice, after he has run away, badly thrashed)*

You see?
It's happened again.
I was trying to be nice,
and he. . . .
But that's always the way it goes:
you try to get them to agree,
and both sides bloody your nose!

*(*THE UNCLEAN *cross the stage, contemptuously elbowing their way through the close-packed ranks of* THE CLEAN, *and sit down around the campfire.* THE CLEAN *stand just behind them, in a circle.)*

PASHA *(stepping forward to stage center)*

True believers!
We must consider what has taken place.
Let us analyze the essence of the phenomenon.

MERCHANT

It's quite simple:
the end of the world has come.

PRIEST

In my opinion, it's the Flood.

CLEMENCEAU

No flood at all.
If so, rain would fall.

RAJA

That's true:
there's been no rain.

DIPLOMAT

So that idea is nonsensical, too.

PASHA

Nonetheless, true believers, what is this event
that has taken place? Let's examine the core.

MERCHANT

I'd say the people have grown disobedient.

GERMAN

I say it's war.

INTELLECTUAL

I disagree.

In my opinion, the cause is quite different.
It's metaphysical, I believe. . . .

MERCHANT *(not satisfied)*

War and the metaphysical!
You're starting with Adam and Eve!

VOICES

One at a time!
One at a time!
Don't start an uproar!

PASHA

Shsh!
Let's keep things dignified!
Student, you have the floor.[6]
(Justifying himself to the crowd)
If not, he'll be fit to be tied.

INTELLECTUAL

At first
everything was simple,
with day following night –
except the sunset red was much too bright.
But then
laws,
ideas,
beliefs,
the granite heaps of the capital cities,
and even the steady red glow of the sun itself –
all things become more fluid, as it were:
somewhat more diluted,
a little bit slipperier.
Then, what a downpour!
The streets were brimful;
melted buildings collapsed on other buildings.
The whole earth,
smelted in the open hearth
of revolution,
poured down like one big waterfall.

VOICE OF THE CHINESE

Attention, ladies and gentlemen!
Here comes the drizzle!

AUSTRALIAN'S WIFE

What do you mean, "drizzle"?
We're already soaked to our bones.

PERSIAN

The end of the world may be at hand,
Yet we hold meetings, orate, and moan.

DIPLOMAT *(snuggling up to the North Pole)*

Come over here and stand
closer together.
It isn't dripping here.

MERCHANT *(kneeing the* ESKIMO HUNTER, *who all this time, with the patience characteristic of his race, has been keeping his finger in the hole in the world)*

Hey, you!
Go join those walruses!

(The HUNTER *runs off, and a stream of water gushes out of the unplugged hole, straight into the faces of those gathered around.* THE CLEAN *scatter to all sides, howling as if with one voice.)*

THE CLEAN

Ee-ee-ee!
Oo-oo-oo!
Ah-ah-ah!

(A moment later they all rush back toward the spout of water.)

Plug that hole!
Stop it up!
Seal it!

(They retreat again. Only the AUSTRALIAN *is left standing beside the terrestrial globe with his finger in the hole. During this general confusion the* RUSSIAN PRIEST *has climbed up on a couple of logs, which serve him as a rostrum.)*

PRIEST

Brothers!
We are losing our last dry place!
The last inch is going under water!

THE UNCLEAN *(in low voices)*

Who's that?
Who's that slob with the beard on his face?

PRIEST

And this will be for forty days and forty nights.

MERCHANT

He's right!
The Lord has inspired him with wisdom!

INTELLECTUAL

There's a precedent – this has happened before.
Remember the famous adventure of Noah?

MERCHANT *(taking the* PRIEST's *place)*

That's so much nonsense –
that history, and all those precedents –

VOICES

Get to the point!

MERCHANT

Brothers, I suggest we build an ark.

THE AUSTRALIAN'S WIFE

That's it! An ark!

THE INTELLECTUAL

What a silly scheme!
What we need is a ship powered by steam.

RAJA

Two steamships!

MERCHANT

That's it!
I'll invest all my capital.
Those others were saved,
and they weren't as clever as we.

GENERAL SHOUT

Hurray!
Long live technology!

MERCHANT

All those in favor
raise their right hands.

GENERAL SHOUT

Useless labor!
You can see our ayes in our eyes.

(Both THE CLEAN *and* THE UNCLEAN *raise their hands.)*

CLEMENCEAU *(taking the place of the* MERCHANT, *and glaring at the* BLACKSMITH, *who has raised his hand)*

What do you think *you're* doing?
Don't start acting wise.
(*To* THE CLEAN)
Gentlemen, let's leave The Unclean behind.
That'll teach them to hold their tongues!

CARPENTER

Can *you* use a hammer and tongs?

CLEMENCEAU *(defeated)*

I've changed my mind.
We'll take The Unclean along.

MERCHANT

But only the sober and the strong.

GERMAN *(stepping up into* CLEMENCEAU'*s place)*

Shsh, gentlemen!
Perhaps we can still avoid dealing with The Unclean.
Fortunately, we don't yet know
what state one-fifth of the world is in.
You make a great din,
but you haven't even bothered to find out
whether we have any Americans about.

MERCHANT *(joyously)*

What a brain! He's no ordinary man.
He's a regular Bismarck!

(His joy is cut short by a cry from the AUSTRALIAN'S WIFE)

What's this?

(Straight out of the orchestra toward the gaping group on stage comes an AMERICAN *on a motorcycle.)*

AMERICAN

Greetings, gentlemen. Say,
is this where they're building the ark?

(He proffers a piece of paper.)

Here's a check for two billion dollars
from the inundated U.S.A.

(There is a silence expressing general discouragement, broken by a cry from the AUSTRALIAN, *who has been holding back the flow of water.)*

AUSTRALIAN

Why are you gaping?

Enough of that!
So help me, I'll pull my fingers out.
They're stiff with cold!

(THE CLEAN *begin bustling about, and huddle close to* THE UNCLEAN.)

CLEMENCEAU *(to the* BLACKSMITH)

Well, comrade, what do you say?
Shall we start building?

BLACKSMITH *(showing no trace of anger)*

Why not?
By me it's OK.

(He crooks a finger at the rest of THE UNCLEAN.)

Come on, comrades!
Let's get going!

(THE UNCLEAN *get to their feet, picking up their saws, planes, and hammers.)*

COMPROMISER

Hurry up, comrades!
Hurry, all you fine lads!
Grab your axes and saws!
Let's all work for the Cause!

INTELLECTUAL *(moving off to one side)*

Work?
I wouldn't dream of it!
I'll just sit right here
and sabotage a bit.

(He shouts to the men at work.)

Faster, men!
Let's make every stroke tell!

CARPENTER

Why do you sit there doing nothing at all?

INTELLECTUAL

I'm a specialist – I'm indispensable.

CURTAIN

ACT II

The deck of the ark. On all sides, a panorama of lands sinking beneath the waves. A mast, with a tangle of cordage resembling a rope ladder, reaches up into the low clouds. On one side is a pilothouse and a hatchway leading down to the ship's hold. THE CLEAN *and* THE UNCLEAN *are grouped along the near side of the ark.*

FARMHAND

Wow! I sure wouldn't want to fall overboard right now!

SEAMSTRESS

Just look at that!
It's no wave – it's a fence!

MERCHANT

Why did I ever get mixed up with you people, anyhow?
It's always that way:
things just don't make sense.
Such sailors you claim to be!
Some sea wolf, I'll say![1]

LAMPLIGHTER

Look! Those waves are so high!
How they howl and sigh!

SEAMSTRESS

That's no fence at all –
we're hemmed in by a wall!

CLEMENCEAU

Yes,
it was very stupid of me.
I tell you this in pain and bitterness.
We should have stayed right where we were.
The world is still quite whole.

And poor thing though it be, the Pole
is still the Pole, nonetheless.

FARMHAND

Why do your wolves
crash like big waves?

BOTH ESKIMOS, THE TRUCK DRIVER, AND THE TWO AUSTRALIANS *(together)*

Look!
What's that?
Where's Alaska? What's happening?

NEGUS

It just flew away
like a stone from a sling.

GERMAN

It went down!

HUNTER

It's gone!

FISHERMAN

All gone!

ALL

Farewell! Farewell! Farewell!

CLEMENCEAU *(overcome by his memories, begins to weep)*

Woe is me!
Woe is me!
I remember how
the whole family
used to gather round the table for tea –
the muffins,
the caviar. . . .

BAKER *(measuring off the end of his fingernail)*

You know, it's funny. But I swear
I don't care
even *that* much!

SHOEMAKER

I've got a little vodka here:
Can you locate a glass?

SERVANT

I'll find one for sure.

MINER

Come on, boys!
Let's go below!

HUNTER

How's the walrus meat?
I hope it's not tough.

SERVANT

Oh, no! Not at all!
Roasted just enough.

(THE CLEAN *are left alone, as* THE UNCLEAN *go down into the hold, singing.)*

THE UNCLEAN

Why be afraid of the flood? What do we have to lose?
We've been tramping around – we've got tired feet.
Heigh, ho! We'll take a rest on this cruise.
No crime in having a drink; no crime eating walrus meat.
Heigh, ho! No crime!

(THE CLEAN *gather around* CLEMENCEAU, *who has been sniveling.)*

PERSIAN

Shame on you!
That's enough of that!

MERCHANT

We'll manage somehow –
we'll make it to Mount Ararat.

NEGUS

You'll starve before you do.

AMERICAN

I've got loads of money on me,
but I'm so hungry I'm half dead.
I'll give a half-million in currency
and two pounds of diamonds
for just one pound of bread.

MERCHANT

I used to speculate, you know –
got arrested three times for it.
But what good is all that money now?

CHINESE

It's not worth a gob of spit!

PASHA

And what good are diamonds?
Today, if a man's got a stone in his bladder
he feels better off –
like his belly was fatter.

AUSTRALIAN

There's no grub at all – just an empty trough.

COMPROMISER

And as if that weren't enough,
they've closed the main market.

MERCHANT *(to the* PRIEST)

Don't worry, humble Father:
today, on every city square
there's a regular country fair.

LADY

Bring your empty pockets instead of jugs,
and fill them with milk and cream and butter!

MERCHANT

You won't get any milk, I can tell you that!
A worker, though, he gets a premium
and payment in kind – things he can barter.

LADY

I'll barter my hats for eggs.

INTELLECTUAL

And when you've bartered your last hat,
you can sit there and suck your thumb!

PRIEST *(listening to the loud noises from the hold)*

What a hubbub!

INTELLECTUAL

No worries for them!
They've caught a fish, and they're gobbling it up.

PRIEST

Let's get a harpoon or a net and do the same.

GERMAN

A h-a-r-p-o-o-n?
I wouldn't know what to do
with one. All I know is how to run a man through
with a sword.

MERCHANT

I threw out a net,

thinking I'd make a nice haul.
I sweated and strained. And what did I get?
Some kelp – so help me, that's all!

PASHA *(dejectedly)*
Things have come to a pretty pass, indeed,
when big merchants have to dine on seaweed!

LLOYD GEORGE *(to* CLEMENCEAU*)*
Eureka!
Let's stop quarreling.
Between a Frenchman and an Englishman,
there just can't be bad blood. The important thing
is that I have a belly, and you have one.

COMPROMISER
Yes, and I have one, too, you know.

CLEMENCEAU
It saddens me
to think that I almost came to blows
with such a fine gentleman!

LLOYD GEORGE
But now fighting's out of the question:
we have a common enemy.
Here is my suggestion.

(He takes CLEMENCEAU *by the arm and leads him aside. After a whispered conference, they come back.)*

CLEMENCEAU
Gentlemen!
Since we are all so immaculate,
is it fitting that we should work and sweat?
Let's make The Unclean work for us.

INTELLECTUAL
I'm all for that!
But what can I do?
I'm delicate.
And each one of them has the strength of two.

LLOYD GEORGE
Oh, there'll be no fighting – God forbid!
We'll have no mayhem.
But while they're gobbling up their meal,
while they're drinking and hollering,

we'll cook up a deal
to betray them.

CLEMENCEAU

We'll give them a king!

COMPROMISER

Why a king? I'd prefer
a commissioner
of police.

CLEMENCEAU

Because the king will hand down a decree
saying, "All foodstuffs belong to me."
So he
will eat, and so will we –
his faithful subjects.

ALL

Wonderful!

PASHA

That hits the mark!

GERMAN *(joyously)*

I told you before –
he's another Bismarck!

AUSTRALIAN

Let's choose him as soon as possible!

SEVERAL VOICES

but who –
who will it be?

LLOYD GEORGE AND CLEMENCEAU

The Negus.

PRIEST

Absolutely!
Let him have the reins!

MERCHANT

What reins?

GERMAN

Why – how is it they say?
"The reins of power" – that's it!
Don't be an idiot.
It's all the same, anyway.
(To the NEGUS*)*
Climb up, my good sir!

LADY

Gentlemen,
tell me: this king –
will he be an impostor,
or the real thing?

VOICES

The real thing! The real thing!

LADY

Oh!
Then I'll be a lady in waiting!

LLOYD GEORGE

Quick!
Hurry and draw up the decree.
"By the grace of God . . ." et cetera,

PASHA AND AUSTRALIAN

And we'll go over there and see
that they don't crawl out.[2]

(The PASHA *and others draw up the decree. The* GERMAN *and the* DIPLOMAT *stretch out a rope in front of the hatch leading to the hold. Staggering,* THE UNCLEAN *emerge. When the last one has clambered out on deck, the* GERMAN *and the* DIPLOMAT *change places, so that* THE UNCLEAN *are bound by the rope.)*

GERMAN *(to the* SHOEMAKER*)*

Hey, you! Come here
and pledge allegiance to the Crown.

SHOEMAKER *(confused)*

Maybe I'd better just lie down.

DIPLOMAT

I'll lie you down
so you won't get up for many a day!
Lieutenant,
point your gun his way![3]

CLEMENCEAU

Aha! They've sobered up!
That makes it simpler.

SEVERAL OF THE UNCLEAN *(sadly)*

Well, boys, we're in the soup!
We're done for!

AUSTRALIAN

Hats off! Who's that
still wearing his hat?

CHINESE *and* RAJA *(nudging the* PRIEST, *who is standing by the wheelhouse, upon which the* NEGUS *has enthroned himself)*

Read it!
Read it quickly, while they're still standing there terrified!

PRIEST *(reading from a scrap of paper)*

By the grace of God, we,
King of all chickens The Unclean have fried,
and Grand Duke of all eggs said chickens have laid,
without ever having flayed
any man seven times (we take only six hides,
and leave the seventh), hereby decree
to our subjects: bring in everything – dried
bread crumbs, fish, porpoises,
and all else that suits our purposes
for eating. The Senate,
without delaying a minute,
will inspect the heap of foodstuffs you bring,
and select the best to regale your King.

PASHA AND RAJA *(forming an improvised Senate)*

We hear and obey, Your Majesty.

PASHA *(giving orders; to the* AUSTRALIAN*)*

You go to the staterooms,
(To the AUSTRALIAN'S WIFE*)*
and you to the storerooms.
(To the whole assemblage)
The Unclean must not eat up the food en route!
(To the MERCHANT, *untying the* BAKER *for him)*
Go down to the hold with him.
The Raja and I will watch things on deck.
Bring the stuff here,
and then go back.

THE CLEAN *(with a shout of joy)*

We'll pile up a mountain of goodies!

PRIEST *(rubbing his hands)*

And then we'll divide the booty,

for such is our Christian duty.

(Under the guard of THE CLEAN, THE UNCLEAN *go down into the hold. In a few minutes they return, and pile up all kinds of edibles in front of the* NEGUS.*)*

MERCHANT *(joyously)*

We cleaned the place out –
didn't leave a thing.
What commodities!
Really a joy!
In a word – rationed stuff.
So whet your teeth, boys!

AMERICAN

What about The Unclean?

GERMAN

They'll have to be locked below.

PRIEST

Well then, let's go!
Wait just a minute, Your Majesty.

(They herd THE UNCLEAN *into the hold. Meanwhile, the* NEGUS *eats up everything that has been brought to him.)*

CLEMENCEAU

Lloyd George, are you coming along?

LLOYD GEORGE

I'm coming, don't worry!

THE CLEAN *(close on one another's heels)*

Hurry! Hurry!
It's time for good cheer!

(They climb up beside the NEGUS. *In front of him is an empty platter.)*

THE CLEAN *(in one menacing voice)*

What's this?
Did a Mongol horde wreak havoc here?

PRIEST *(furious)*

How could one lone man munch
all that much?

PASHA

I'd like to give him one good punch
in that bulging mug!

NEGUS

Silence! I'm anointed of the Lord on High!

GERMAN

Anointed? Anointed?
If you had to try. . . .

DIPLOMAT

To sleep on an empty belly, like us. . . .

PRIEST

Judas!

RAJA

Ugh!
I never thought I'd see such a day!

MERCHANT

Let's lie down,
and take counsel of our pillow, as they say.

(They lie down. Night. The moon moves swiftly across the sky, and disappears. Dawn. In the gray first light, the DIPLOMAT *raises himself on his elbow. On the other side, the* GERMAN *does the same.)*

DIPLOMAT

You asleep?

(The GERMAN *shakes his head in the negative.)*

Why so early awake?

GERMAN

How could I sleep,
with my belly rumbling like an earthquake?
Well, come on, talk some more!

COMPROMISER

I kept dreaming of steak.

PRIEST *(from a distance)*

What else could you possibly have dreamed about?

(Pointing to the NEGUS*)*

A curse on him! He looks so sleek!

AUSTRALIAN

It's cold.

INTELLECTUAL *(indicating the* NEGUS*)*

He has no spiritual doubts.
He's eaten his fill, and he's happy that way.

CLEMENCEAU *(after a brief pause)*
Gentlemen, do you know what?
I believe I've turned democrat.

GERMAN
Well, you don't say!
As for me,
I've always loved the People passionately.

PERSIAN *(with venom)*
And who was it proposed we pledge faith to His Majesty?

DIPLOMAT
No more poisonous barbs, gentlemen!
Autocracy, as a form of government,
is undoubtedly obsolete.

MERCHANT
It certainly is, if there's nothing to eat!

GERMAN
Seriously, gentlemen! Seriously!
Revolution is hatching.
Let's bury the hatchet.
and keep things friendly.

COMPROMISER
Hurray!
Hurray for the Constituent Assembly!

ALL *(opening the hatch)*
Hurray!
Hurray!
(To one another)
Yo, heave, ho!
Hew away!
(THE UNCLEAN, *awakened, climb out of the hatch.)*

SHOEMAKER
What's this? Too much drinking?

BLACKSMITH
Are we sinking?

MERCHANT
Citizens, please come to the meeting.
(To the BAKER*)*
Citizen, are you for a republic?

THE UNCLEAN *(in chorus)*

A meeting?
A republic?
What's that?

CLEMENCEAU

Wait right there. The intellectual
will explain some things that affect you all.
(To the INTELLECTUAL*)*
Hey, you, Intellectual!
(The INTELLECTUAL *and* CLEMENCEAU *climb up on the wheelhouse.)*
I declare the Assembly in session!
(To the INTELLECTUAL*)*
You have the floor.

INTELLECTUAL

Citizens!
That great big King has a mouth that's incredible!

VOICES

True!
True, Citizen Orator!

INTELLECTUAL

He'll gobble up every existing thing that's edible –
the rat!

VOICE

True!

INTELLECTUAL

And nobody will ever reach Ararat!

VOICES

Verily!
Verily!

INTELLECTUAL

We've had enough of that!
Break your rusty chains!

GENERAL ROAR

Down with him! Down with autocracy!

COMPROMISER

Who is it you're threatening?
Aha!
The King!

You'll spend the rest of your lives on a convict's plank bed!
The King's power is from God – it's sacred.
Don't touch it! Why not agree,
gentlemen,
to a constitutional monarchy
under the Grand Duke Michael or Nicholas?

THE CLEAN AND THE UNCLEAN *(together)*

Don't be ridiculous!
Agree?
So he can devour everything?

GERMAN

I'll agree you, all right!

ALL *(in chorus)*

We'll give you with your agreeing!

COMPROMISER *(having been thrashed; plaintively)*

How steamed up they've become!
And how quarrelsome!
It's easier to die
than to make them see eye to eye.

MERCHANT *(to the* NEGUS*)*

You've drunk up our blood!
You've cheated the People monstrously!

CLEMENCEAU *(to the* NEGUS*)*

Hey, you!
Allons enfants into the sea!

(They ALL *grab the* NEGUS, *swing him back and forth a few times, and heave him overboard. Then* THE CLEAN *lock arms with* THE UNCLEAN, *pairing off, and they disperse, whispering.)*

DIPLOMAT *(to the* MINER*)*

Comrades,
you just can't imagine how
delighted I am!
No more of those age-old barriers now!

CLEMENCEAU *(to the* BLACKSMITH*)*

Congratulations!
Ancient social foundations
have collapsed.

BLACKSMITH *(noncommittally)*
Uhm! So I see.

CLEMENCEAU
The rest will arrange itself easily;
the rest is a snap.

PRIEST *(to the* SEAMSTRESS*)*
Now we're for you, and you're for us.

MERCHANT *(pleased)*
That's the way! Lead 'em by the nose!

LADY
How could anyone really believe
I was hot for the Negus? I live and breathe
only for the Constituent;
for the Provisional Government –
or whatever you want!
I'll even go around pregnant
for two whole years! Meanwhile,
I'll make haste to put on my red ribbons.
(One must, after all, keep up with the Revolutionary style!)
But I'll return in a minute – no more! –
To the People I so adore.
(She runs off to her hatboxes.)

CLEMENCEAU *(on the wheelhouse)*
Well, citizens, that's enough.
You've romped to your heart's content.
Now let's set up our democratic government.
Citizens,
in order to make this easy and quick,
we (God rest the Negus' soul!) – the thirteen of us –
will be ministers and deputy ministers;
and you – citizens of a democratic republic –
will bake rolls, make boots, and hunt walrus.
Are there any demurs?
Are these policies approved by all here?

FARMHAND
Sure,
just as long as the water's near.

ALL *(in chorus)*
Long live our democratic republic!

CLEMENCEAU (*to* THE UNCLEAN)

And now I propose that you get to work.

(To THE CLEAN*)*

And you – take pen in hand.

[*To* THE UNCLEAN *again*]

Get to work, and bring in what you can.
We'll divide it equally with you:
the last shirt will be torn in two.

(THE CLEAN *set up a table and begin fussing with documents. When* THE UNCLEAN *bring in edibles, the former enter them as "Merchandise Received"; then, as soon as* THE UNCLEAN *leave, they consume the food with gusto. The* BAKER, *on his second trip back, tries to see what is under some of the documents.)*

LLOYD GEORGE

Why are you peeking?
Stand back from those documents!
This work is above your level of intelligence.

CLEMENCEAU

You don't understand a whit
about governmental administration.
Each incoming plate,
and each outgoing one,
must have a number assigned to it.

BLACKSMITH

Before you get all those numbers on,
The Unclean may be dead and gone.

BAKER

You promised to share – so let's!

PRIEST *(worried)*

Brethren!
It's too soon to think of food yet.

RAJA *(leading* THE UNCLEAN *away from the table)*

Look – a shark!
They just caught one there.
Does it lay eggs
or give milk, I wonder?

BLACKSMITH

Listen, Raja, or Pasha, or whatever you are!

Remember that saying they have in Turkey:
"Pasha, don't push us too far!"
(Returning, with the rest of THE UNCLEAN*)*
They're learning things!
You can try and try
to milk a shark, but she'll always be dry.

SHOEMAKER *(to those who are writing at the table)*
It's time to eat. Quick! Finish your work!

AMERICAN
Just take a look!
How beautiful –
the waves and the gull!

FARMHAND
We'd do better to talk about soup and tea.
Let's have some chow!
No time for gulls now.

CLEMENCEAU
Look! Look!
There's a whale
on the sea!

SOLDIER OF THE RED ARMY
To hell with the whale!
You're a whale yourself!

THE UNCLEAN *(in chorus, overturning the table)*
Get out of here with your bureaucracy!
(The empty plates fall to the deck with a crash.)

SEAMSTRESS AND LAUNDRESS *(sadly)*
The government has licked the plates clean!

CARPENTER *(leaping up on the overturned table)*
Comrades, this is a knife in the back!

VOICES
And a fork to boot!

MINER
Comrades, what's this?
Before, one mouth chawed; now a regiment chaws.
The republic turned out to be the same thing
as a king –
but one with a hundred jaws.

CLEMENCEAU *(picking his teeth)*
Why so excited?

We promised to share things equally,
and we've done it:
one man gets the ring of the doughnut,
the other man gets the core.
That's what a democratic republic is for.

MERCHANT

Not everyone
can have the melon:
somebody has to take the seeds.

THE UNCLEAN

What this country needs
is a good class struggle. We'll show you one!

COMPROMISER

Once again!
Once again the roof is falling in!
Once again we have chaos and uproar.
Enough! Enough!
Don't start spilling blood!
Listen, please!
I can't take any more!
That's all very good –
the Commune, and so on –
but it will take centuries.
Comrade workers! You must seek
an accord with The Clean. Take the advice
of an old, experienced Menshevik.

LLOYD GEORGE

Accord?
Why, I'd lose all my capital!
We'll give you with your accord!

SOLDIER OF THE RED ARMY

I'll accord you, all right!

COMPROMISER

My position is miserable!
Once again I'm besieged from both sides!

(THE UNCLEAN *crowd in on* THE CLEAN)

THE CLEAN

Hold, citizens! Our policy –

THE UNCLEAN

Come on!

We'll roast 'em on four sides – not just two!
We'll show 'em a policy to remember!
Stand fast, damn you![4]
You'll never forget the Seventh of November![5]

*(*THE UNCLEAN *arm themselves with the weapons laid aside by* THE CLEAN *while they were eating. They drive* THE CLEAN *to the stern. There is a glimpse of the latter's heels as they are tossed overboard. But the* MERCHANT, *grabbing half of a roasted walrus, hides in a chest in one corner. The* INTELLECTUAL *and the* LADY *hide in another. The* COMPROMISER *takes the* FARMHAND *by the arm, trying to lead him away, and sobbing meanwhile.)*

FARMHAND

What a bastard!
Couldn't make up his mind.
All he could do was stand there and drool.
Revolution, fine sir, isn't Sunday school![6]

(The COMPROMISER *bites the* FARMHAND *in the arm.)*

BLACKSMITH

What a nasty temper!
Come on, boys, let's come give him the old heave-ho down below!

(They throw the COMPROMISER *down into the hold.)*

CHIMNEY SWEEP

He might choke for air down there.
He's just like a woman. For all that fat,
he's still delicate.

FARMHAND

Let's not hem and haw and hem!
If they came back,
they'd nail all of us up on the cross.
If we take it easy on them,
they'll get Ararat for sure!

THE UNCLEAN

That's right! That's right!
It's either them or us!

FARMHAND

Make way for the reign of terror!

BLACKSMITH

Sure, comrades,
kick the weaklings over the side!
But come, lads, why don't you raise up a cheer?
Let's cheer!

(But the voices of THE UNCLEAN *are stern; the Republic ate up the last food supplies.)*

BAKER

Cheer?
Have you thought about bread? Or grain?

FARMHAND

Cheer?
And where could we plant grain, anyway?

LAMPLIGHTER

Cheer?
With no furrowed fields – only troughs in the waves?

FISHERMAN

Cheer?
We've got nothing to fish with – our nets are torn.

TRUCK DRIVER

How can a man get across that water?
If we just had some dry land near!

HUNTER

There's a leak in the ark!

TRUCK DRIVER

There's no compass!

ALL

Disaster has struck!

BLACKSMITH

We're halfway there – we mustn't stop!
The food that went down
the throats of those people that drowned,
can't be brought back up.
There's just one thing, now, we must all aim at:
to keep our strength till we reach Ararat.
Let the storms lash us!
Let the sun scorch us!
Let hunger come!

We'll look it straight in the eye.
We may eat nothing more than sea foam.
Still, everything here is our own!

LAUNDRESS

We'll eat today,
but tomorrow's the end!
Only two biscuits left in the whole ark.

FARMHAND

Hey!
Comrades!
Unless a man shows his rationing card,
don't give out biscuits!

(The INTELLECTUAL *and the* LADY *peek out from the chest in the corner.)*

INTELLECTUAL

Hark!
They're saying, "Give out biscuits!"
while *we* suffer cold and hunger and all kinds of torments.

LADY

Let's enter the employ of the Soviet Government.

(They crawl out.)

THE UNCLEAN

What's this? Weren't they dunked in the Big Pond?
Are they returnees from the Great Beyond?

INTELLECTUAL

By no means.
We're on your team.
We're not Party members;
we're from the corner chest.
But we're for the regime
of the Soviets.

LADY

I loathe the middle class!
Those swindlers!
I was just waiting to see
how long it would be
before the middle class collapsed.
If you'll allow me,
I, too,

will work for you
as a typist —
even if I have to hunt and peck.

INTELLECTUAL

Take me, too.
It's bad not having a specialist.
Without one,
where can you turn?
Just one way: down —
meaning you're sunk.

BLACKSMITH

We won't sink.
Don't caw like a crow
announcing doom.
(To the LADY*)*
Comrade, have a seat.
(To the INTELLECTUAL*)*
Get down below
and take charge of the boiler room!

TRUCK DRIVER

A man without food
is like an old locomotive without wood.

MINER

Even I'm giving up — and I'm a strong man.

SOLDIER OF THE RED ARMY

It wasn't enough just to kill off The Clean.
We need bread.
And we have to get water, too.

THE UNCLEAN

What can we try?
What can we do?

SEAMSTRESS

The good Lord can't let us die.
Let's fold our hands and wait.

HUNTER

One muscle after another
is weakening from hunger.

SEAMSTRESS *(listening)*

What's that?
Do you hear it?

Do you hear the music?

CARPENTER

It was the Antichrist who told us those tales
of Paradise and Ararat!
(Jumps up, frightened, and points out to sea.)
Who is that
walking over the waves,
rolling his own bones?

CHIMNEY SWEEP

Stop that fuss!
The ocean is bare.
Besides, who could show up there?

SHOEMAKER

Here he comes. . . .
It's Famine,
coming to break his fast on us!

FARMHAND

Well, let him come!
None of us here are ready to die.
Comrades, the enemy is alongside!
All hands on deck!
Famine himself
is about to attack!
(They come on the run, tottering, armed with anything handy. It grows light. A pause.)

ALL

Well, come on then! . . .
There's nobody! . . .
So once again
we'll look out at the barren waste of the sea.

HUNTER

Thus when, in the desert's fiery heat, praying for shade,
a man lies dying,
and the sands appear to cool, it's a mirage – made
by his own eyes, lying.

TRUCK DRIVER *(getting very excited, adjusts his glasses, looks out to sea; to the* BLACKSMITH*)*

Over there,
to the west –
don't you see that little speck?

BLACKSMITH

Why look?
You might just as well hang your specs
on your tail, or smash them on a rock.[7]

TRUCK DRIVER *(runs off to one side, rummages around, then, taking a spyglass, climbs up to the yardarm. A moment later he shouts, his voice quivering with joy)*

Ararat! Ararat! Ararat!

ALL *(from all sides)*

I'm so glad!
I'm so glad!

(They snatch the spyglass from the TRUCK DRIVER *and huddle together.)*

CARPENTER

Where is it?

BLACKSMITH

Over there.
You can see it
just off to the right.

CARPENTER

What's happening?
It's raising itself.
It's standing upright.
It's walking!

TRUCK DRIVER

What do you mean, "walking"?
Ararat is a mountain – it can't walk.
Rub your eyes!

CARPENTER

Rub your own!
Just look!

TRUCK DRIVER

Yes, it *is* walking!
It's some kind of a human.
Yes, a man.
An old man with a cane.
A young man without a cane.
Say! He walks on the water like it was dry land!

SEAMSTRESS

O bells, ring out!

Peal joyously!
For it
is He
who walked the waters of Galilee!

BLACKSMITH

God has oranges,
cherries,
and apples;
He can make spring leaf out seven times in one day.
But from us He has always turned away.
And now He's sent Christ here to snare us.

FARMHAND

We don't want Him.
Don't let that crook come near us!
Hungry men's mouths don't need to pray.
Stop right there, you,
or I'll let you have it!
Say,
who are you anyway?

(A most ordinary young MAN *steps up onto the frozen deck.)*

MAN

Who am I?
I'm of no class,
no tribe,
no clan.
I've seen the Thirtieth Century
and the Fortieth.
I'm simply the man
of the future.
I came to fan
the flames in the forges of souls,
for I know
how hard it is
to try to live.
Listen!
A new
Sermon on the Mount.
Are you waiting for Ararats?
There aren't any Ararats — none!

They're just something you saw in a fit
of dreaming.
And if the mountain doesn't come
to Muhammad, then to hell with it!
Far be it from me
to preach of a Christian Heaven
where fasting fools lap up unsweetened tea.
The Heaven I'm shouting about
is a genuine, earthly one.
Judge for yourselves: Is it like Christ's,
or the famine-struck Heaven of the Apostles?
In my heavenly house are many mansions – crammed
with furniture –
and the stylish comfort and ease made possible
by electrical fixtures.
There, labor is sweet, and won't callus your hands;
work will bloom in your palms like a rose.
There, the sun will perform such miracles
that at every step
you will sink down in flower beds big as the sea.
Here, one must toil endlessly,
using all of the gardener's skill
(the glass frame, the manure mixed with soil).
There,
pineapples will grow six times a year
from the root of the common dill.

ALL *(in chorus)*

We'll all go!
What's there to lose?
But will sinners like us
be let in?

MAN

My Paradise is for everyone
except the poor in spirit,
who are swollen up as big as the moon
from fasting in Lent.
A camel can pass through the eye of a needle more easily
than such an elephant
can enter my kingdom.
Come unto me

all you who have calmly stabbed the enemy,
and then walked away from his corpse
with a song on your lips!
Come,
unforgiving one!
You have first right of entry
into my kingdom –
which is earthly, not heavenly!
Come all
who are not pack mules,
and all
for whom life is cruel
and unbearable!
My kingdom – earthly, not heavenly –
is for you.

ALL *(in chorus)*

Isn't he mocking the poor?
[*To the* MAN]
Where and what are they –
those great lands with which you tease us?

MAN

Long is the way.
We must pass through the clouds.

ALL *(in chorus)*

We'll smash every cloud to pieces!

MAN

And if Hell is piled upon Hell?

ALL *(in chorus)*

Then we'll go there as well.
We won't turn back.
Lead us!
Where is it?

MAN

Where?
You're waiting for somebody else to tell.
Meanwhile, it's right here
within reach.
What are you doing with it?
Where are your hands?
They're idle – you've folded them.

You're huddled together like beggars.
But you're rich men!
Just look around you – what wealth!
How dares the wind toy with the ark?
Away with Nature's insufferable yoke!
You will live in warmth
and light, having made electricity
move in waves. And even if you are cast
down to the depths, have no dread:
the floor of the sea
is more fair
than a meadow. Our daily bread –
sea coal – grows there.
Let the winds blow up a flood!
Let the sides of the ark split wide!
The left hand and the right –
these two
will save you.
I've finished.
You have the floor.
I'll say no more.

(He disappears. On deck, excitement and bewilderment)

SHOEMAKER

Where is he?

BLACKSMITH

I think he's in me.

FARMHAND

He managed to crawl inside me, too, I think.

VOICES

Who is he?
Who is that free spirit?
Who is he –
that nameless one?
Who is he,
with no country of his own?
Why did he come?
What prophecies did he utter?
On every hand
is the deadly bath of the flood.

No matter!
We'll still find the Promised Land!

FARMHAND

So Heaven exists after all!
And it's really not stupid to try
for happiness!

VOICES

So that we can get there faster,
raise your hammers high!
Lift up your axes!
Dress ranks!
The ark is cracking!
Salvation lies in discipline.

BLACKSMITH *(with one hand on a yardarm)*

The gaping maw of the gulf bodes ill.
Only one path remains:
through the clouds!
Forward!

(They all rush to the mast.)

ALL *(in chorus)*

Through the sky – forward!

(From the yardarms, their battle song rings out.)

Hey, up the shrouds!
Up the shrouds, hey!
Up the shrouds and away,
commissars of the seas!
Forward, commissars of the seas!

SHOEMAKER

There the victors can rest up after the fray.
Though our feet may be tired, we'll make shoes from the sky.

ALL *(in chorus)*

We'll make shoes!
For our bleeding feet, we'll make shoes from the sky!

CARPENTER

Heaven's gates are flung wide!
Up and in we will go!
Up ladders of sunbeams
and stairs of rainbows!

ALL *(in chorus)*

Up ladders of sunbeams
and swings of rainbows!

FISHERMAN

Enough prophets we've seen!
We're all Nazarenes!
Climb up the masts!
Grab hold of the yards!

ALL *(in chorus)*

To the masts!
To the masts!
To the shrouds!
To the shrouds!

(When the last of THE UNCLEAN *has disappeared, the* LADY *and the* INTELLECTUAL *climb up the shrouds after them. The* COMPROMISER *stands for a moment, reflecting.)*

COMPROMISER

Where are you going?
To the Commune?
You're crazy to go all that way!

(He looks around him. The ark makes a cracking sound.)

Forward, comrades. Better ahead
than dead!

(The COMPROMISER *disappears. Finally the* MERCHANT *crawls out of his corner chest, smirking.)*

MERCHANT

Are *they* ever dumb!
This property here I'd estimate
at a minimum
of four million – even as scrap.
Well, I'll speculate.
What's that?
It's breaking up!
It's cracking!
Abandon ship!
We're sinking!
Comrades! Comrades!
Wait a minute,

comrades!
I'm in the throes
of perishing here all alone!

COMPROMISER

Come along! Come along!
You might get a concession – who knows?

CURTAIN

ACT III

Hell. A huge doorway. Above it a sign: "NO ADMITTANCE WITHOUT HAVING BEEN ANNOUNCED." *Along the sides of the stage,* GUARD DEVILS. *Two* MESSENGER DEVILS *call to each other across the theater. From behind the door, onstage, low singing is heard.*[1]

CHORUS

Devils! Devils! Devils are we!
The souls of miserable sinners
we rotate on our rotisserie!

FIRST MESSENGER

It's a lousy life, brother Devil.

SECOND MESSENGER

Yeah. These past few months have been hard on me.

FIRST MESSENGER

In a word,
it's strictly third
category.[2]

CHORUS

Down on earth, they've chased out the priests —
those grafters in cassocks. That's all very well;
but now nobody sends us sinners to eat,
so *we've* got a food shortage, too, here in Hell.

SECOND MESSENGER

Since those devils they call The Clean
arrived on the scene,
we natives are just getting skinnier and skinnier.
"Serve me this! Serve me that!" they say.

FIRST MESSENGER

The worst is that Negus of Abyssinia!

That black mug!
He eats like a pig!

CHORUS

Alack! Well-a-day! Alack! Well-a-day!
If we don't get some food we'll all croak right away!

FIRST MESSENGER

Before,
every devil's cheeks bulged like watermelons.

SECOND MESSENGER

That's right.

FIRST MESSENGER

But no more!
Since they chased out the priests, not one middleman have we had!

SECOND MESSENGER

The rations are slight.

FIRST MESSENGER

And they're lousy!

SECOND MESSENGER

It wouldn't be so bad
if these new devils were of the right sort.
But they're disgusting: all bald,
with their tails cut short!

FIRST MESSENGER

You just wait. Pretty soon
we'll have our own revolution.

SECOND MESSENGER

Shsh! There's the doorbell again!

(They leap clear across the stage. The GUARDS *question the* MESSENGERS. *Then, having made a brief report, they throw open the doors.* [*Enter* LLOYD GEORGE, CLEMENCEAU, *the* PASHA, *the* GERMAN, *the* PRIEST, *the* CHINESE, *the* NEGUS, *and various other devils.*])

LLOYD GEORGE

Some devils you are!
Some fiends, I declare!
Why don't some sinners fall into your snare?

PRIEST *(shaking his fist at the* MESSENGERS)

Was it for this that I served you so well?

To have my food rationed in Hell?

MESSENGERS *(sullenly)*

Maybe you two
should grab pitchforks and go hunting, too.

CLEMENCEAU

Shut up!
No more of that!
We're blue-blooded devils.
You fiends of the proletariat
must labor, sparing no sweat,
for those from the higher social levels.

SECOND MESSENGER

They've brought their own system with 'em.
Now we've got class antagonism
among devils, yet!

PASHA

So you still want to gab?
Still spoiling for strife?
I'll give you a jab
with my fork – or my knife!

MASTER-OF-CEREMONIES DEVIL

His Highness, Beelzebub, intends
to say a few words to his faithful subjects.

GERMAN

All rise!
Attention!
Don't wiggle your rear ends!

BEELZEBUB *(entering)*

My devils loyal and true!
Your days of hunger are through!
Shout with merriment!
Hoist your tails on high!
The end of our fasting, the end of Lent,
is nigh.
Fifteen sinners or more are coming this way.

PRIEST *(crossing himself)*

Thank God!
No more singing of masses on curds and whey!

CHINESE

They've a businesslike look, this new lot,

even though they are sans-culottes.

NEGUS

Aha! Now I'll gorge till my gut has swelled!
Even the devils will be repelled!

LLOYD GEORGE

And I'll sharpen my horns. Just you wait and see!
I'll teach them to overthrow *me!*

BEELZEBUB *(to the* MESSENGERS)

Get to your lookout posts
on the double!
Here, take your binoculars.
Look sharp, and make sure
that not one gets away.
If there's any trouble,
there'll be Hell to pay!

(The MESSENGERS, *taking their binoculars, run off the stage and into the orchestra, listening. The door flies open.)*

FIRST MESSENGER

Just so they come in, and don't pass by!
I'll give 'em what's for!
I'll raise my tail high,
and lower my horns!

SECOND MESSENGER

It'll be a fright!

FIRST MESSENGER

I'll fix 'em, all right!
They'll wish they'd never been born!
One of my favorite dinners
is a stew made of juicy sinners.

SECOND MESSENGER

I'll eat 'em as is –
not in a hash.
Shsh! Do you hear it?
Crash, bang, crash!
Crash, bang, crash!

(He listens. One can hear the racket made by THE UNCLEAN *as they smash up Limbo.)*

FIRST MESSENGER

The chief will love this!

SECOND MESSENGER

Shut up!
Cut the gaff!
Run and notify Beelzebub
and his staff.

(The FIRST MESSENGER *runs off.* BEELZEBUB *climbs to the middle tier of the clouds.*[3] *He shades his eyes with one hand. All the* DEVILS *rise to their feet.)*

BEELZEBUB *(after having checked the situation, yells)*

Hey, you devils!
Bring in the caldrons!
And let's have more wood for the fire –
thicker pieces, and dryer.
Then form a squadron
and hide in a cloud.
Not a single sinner must be allowed
to escape!

(The DEVILS *hide. From below one hears:* "To the masts! To the masts! To the shrouds! To the shrouds!" *Then the mob of* THE UNCLEAN *surges in, followed a moment later by the* DEVILS, *with their pitchforks held at the ready.)*

DEVILS

Ooh-ooh-ooh-ooh!
Ah-ah-ah-ah!

BLACKSMITH *(to the* SEAMSTRESS, *pointing to the front rank of the* DEVILS *and laughing)*

We've seen the likes of them before!
What do you make of 'em, eh?
We dealt with the devils without any horns,
and we'll deal with this crew the same way!

(The racket made by the DEVILS *begins to grow tiresome.* THE UNCLEAN *hiss.)*

THE UNCLEAN

S-s-s-s-s-s-!

(The DEVILS, *confused, quiet down.)*

Is this Hell?

DEVILS *(uncertainly)*

Y-yes.

FARMHAND *(gesturing toward Purgatory*[4]*)*
Comrades,
don't stop!
We'll go
straight ahead!

BEELZEBUB
Is that so?
Devils, forward!
Don't let them get into Purgatory!

FARMHAND
Just listen to that oratory!

BLACKSMITH *(to* BEELZEBUB*)*
Oh, come off it!

BEELZEBUB *(affronted)*
"Come off it!" did you say?

BLACKSMITH
I did.
You should be ashamed –
an old devil like you,
with gray hairs on your head.
As if you could scare us that way!
Have you ever visited
a foundry, by any chance?

BEELZEBUB *(stiffly)*
A foundry? I've not had the pleasure.

BLACKSMITH
Just as I thought!
If you had,
you'd have shed your fur.
In this place you live like some fancy-pants.
So sleek! Yet you act so tough!

BEELZEBUB
I'll give you with *sleek!*
I'll give you with *tough!*
We've talked enough!
Into the flames you go!

BLACKSMITH
Is that so?
Think you'll frighten us good?
What a laugh!

In Moscow they'd pay you for all that firewood.
There, people get sick from the freezing weather.
But the temperature's fine here in Hell.
It's a seventh heaven:
you all go around *au naturel.*

BEELZEBUB
Enough of your jokes!
Tremble for your souls. Without more ado,
we're going to suffocate all of you
with sulfur!

BLACKSMITH *(getting angry)*
What a bluffer!
You brag a lot –
but what have you really got?
A whiff of sulfur, that's all!
On earth, when they use poison gas,
whole regiments fall
like clipped grass,
and the plain turns gray with the coats of the dead.

BEELZEBUB
I warn you – beware of the red-hot caldron!
Soon you'll be sprawled on
the prongs of a pitchfork.
Your fate is precarious!

FARMHAND *(beside himself)*
Why all this yacking
about some old pitchforks?
Your stupid Hell is like honey to us!
Sometimes, in the war,
when we were attacking,
three men out of four
would be cut down
by one burst of machine-gun fire.
(The DEVILS *prick up their ears.)*

BEELZEBUB *(struggling to maintain discipline)*
Why do you stand there
and stare?
Perhaps he's a liar.

FARMHAND *(furious)*
I'm *lying?*

You stay here in your caves
like varmints. . . .
Devils, listen!
Let me tell you –

DEVILS

Silence!

FARMHAND

. . . about our earthly torments.
What does Beelzebub amount to,
with his pitchfork, strolling around Hell?
I'll invite you to earth for a spell.
Devils, do you know what a siege can be?
(As if some old pitchforks could frighten *us!*) Well,
we workers were entertained handsomely
by British tanks. And Capital,
with a pincers of squadrons and armies, squeezed
the Workers' Republic. Here, at least,
you don't have any children or righteous men.
(If you did, would you really torture them?)
But on earth they are tortured along with the rest.
No, devils,
it's better here.
True, like some savage Turk, you take
a sinner and set him down hard on the stake,
while we have machinery,
we have culture –

VOICE *(from among the* DEVILS*)*

Really?

FARMHAND

You drink blood. So what?
It's tasteless raw.
If I had the time, I'd show you a plant
where blood is refined into chocolate
for the bourzhwaw.

VOICE *(from among the* DEVILS*)*

Wha-at?
Seriously?

FARMHAND

And if you devils got just one look
at a slave from a British colony,

you'd squeal and run off to all sides.
They flay the Negroes and tan their hides
so they can be used to bind books.
You drive spikes in men's ears?
What for?
They force hog bristles under the fingernails.
And you should see how a soldier fares
in the trenches. Compared to him,
your martyr is only a lazy bum.

VOICE *(from among the* DEVILS*)*

No more!
It makes my fur stand on end!
These stories leave me numb!

FARMHAND

And you think we're scared?
So you've kindled your fires!
So you've hung your pots up!
Fine devils you are!
Why, you're no more than pups!
Ever worked in a factory and had your joints stretched
by a driving belt?

BEELZEBUB *(flustered)*

Just listen to them!
When in Rome
they do just as they do at home.

PRIEST *(nudging* BEELZEBUB*)*

Go ahead!
Tell them about the fiery furnace.

BEELZEBUB

I tried,
but they wouldn't listen.
My hands are tied.

FARMHAND *(advancing toward* BEELZEBUB*)*

So it's only the cowards you bare your fangs at!

BEELZEBUB

Can't you just leave me alone?
A devil's a devil, and that's that.

COMPROMISER *(trying to keep the* DEVILS *and* THE UNCLEAN *apart)*

Oh, Lord!

Here we go again!
[*To* THE UNCLEAN]
What's the matter –
aren't two revolutions enough?
Gentlemen! Comrades!
Don't start any rough stuff!
[*To the* DEVILS]
Don't you have anything better to eat?
This is some pie you've got!
[*To* THE UNCLEAN]
And you're a fine lot –
never willing to dicker!
He's an old and respected devil, as you can see.
You must learn not to bicker.
The thing to do is agree.

BEELZEBUB

You little bootlicker!

FARMHAND

You snake!
(The COMPROMISER *is belabored by both parties.)*

COMPROMISER *(appealing to the audience)*

Citizens, I ask you:
Is this a fair shake?
I call upon them to agree,
and both of them give it to me!

BEELZEBUB *(sadly)*

I'd ask you to stay and have dinner,
but what could I serve? Just skin and bones.
You know what people are like of late:
a man, well roasted,
makes a mere speck on your plate.
A few days ago they brought in one
who'd worked in the cesspools! Phew!
Yes, it's sad to relate,
but we've nothing to offer you.

FARMHAND *(contemptuously)*

Go to your devils!
(To THE UNCLEAN, *who have been waiting impatiently)*
Comrades, let's go!

(THE UNCLEAN *start to move onward and upward;* BEELZEBUB *buttonholes the last one.)*

BEELZEBUB

Bon voyage! And don't forget
I'm a devil that's highly qualified.
When you're all set,
send for me,
and I'll head up the Main Fuel Agency.
Here, we sit and suffer the throes
of hunger – sometimes for as long as five days
and five nights;
and devils, as everyone knows,
have devilish appetites!

(THE UNCLEAN *move upward. Shattered clouds fall. Darkness. From the darkness and the chaos of the now empty stage the following scene emerges. Meantime, the singing of* THE UNCLEAN *resounds through Hell.)*

BLACKSMITH

Throw yourselves forward
and break down the portals of Hell!
Smash Purgatory to bits!
Onward!
Fear not!

ALL *(in chorus)*

Smash Purgatory to smithereens!
Hey!
Fear not!

MINER

Forward!
Our bodies must learn how to do without rest.
To the cloud banks!
Higher!
Walk on the clouds!

ALL *(in chorus)*

Walk on the cloud banks!
Higher!
To the clouds!

(The LADY *appears out of nowhere and throws herself on* BEELZEBUB*'s breast.)*

LADY

Beelzebubchik!
Darling!
My own!
Don't let me perish all alone!
Let me in!
Take me in with your people!
Let me in, sweet!
The Unclean are such a rough lot!

BEELZEBUB

I'll grant you asylum –
why not?
Just step over this way.

(He gestures toward the door, from which a moment later two DEVILS *with pitchforks leap forth. Seizing the* LADY, *they drag her away.* BEELZEBUB *rubs his hands.)*

Well, that's one at least.
It's always pleasant to feast
on a deserter.

CURTAIN

ACT IV

Paradise. Clouds are piled upon clouds. A whitish atmosphere. Center stage, the DWELLERS IN PARADISE *are seated on a cloud mass.* METHUSELAH *is making a speech.*

METHUSELAH

Most saintly ones!
Go to the sun deck and straighten the relics!
Polish the days a bit more.
Gabriel says
that a dozen or more
of the righteous are on their way here.
Most saintly ones!
Receive them among you.
Like a cat toying with a mouse,
hunger
torments them; and the sight of Hell
has made them sick. Yet still they toil
onward.

DWELLERS IN PARADISE *(solemnly)*

It is plain they deserve to be honored.
We will receive them. We will not fail
to make them welcome.

METHUSELAH

We must set the table,
and then go to greet them at the door.
A solemn reception is called for.

DWELLERS IN PARADISE

As the oldest, you be master of ceremonies.

METHUSELAH

But I'm not able –

ALL

Please, please!

METHUSELAH *(bows, then goes about making arrangements at the table and assigning places)*

Chrysostom,
over here!
Make ready a speech of welcome.
"We welcome you, as does Christ . . ."
and so on. But you know best
how to do these things.
Over here, Tolstoy!
You're the handsomest:
your appearance is decorative.
Just stay as you are.
(It's too late to change, anyway.)
This way,
Rousseau!
Now you others deploy
in a line, while I go
to inspect the table. . . . My son,
are you milking the cloud?

ANGEL

Yes, sir.

METHUSELAH

Well, when you're done,
set the milk on the table, and then
start carving. One morsel of cloud apiece
will suffice.
For saints, the main thing isn't eatables,
but the lofty discourse that flows at the table.

SAINTS

Well,
aren't they in view yet?
The edge of that cloud has begun to swell
suspiciously.
Here they come! Here they come!
Can it really be they?
They're in Paradise, yet they have the look
of chimney sweeps covered with soot.
We'll scrub it away.

Umh. Not all saints, one would gather,
are of the same feather.

THE UNCLEAN *(from below)*

Make your rifles shout!
Make your cannons roar!
We ourselves are Christ and Savior!

(They break through the cloud floor and swarm in; in chorus)

Ugh! Look at those guys with the beards!
Three hundred or more!

METHUSELAH

Come in! Come in!
Glad to have you aboard!

ANGEL'S VOICE

They've let in a crazy brood!

ANGELS

Howdy do! Howdy do! Make yourselves at home!

METHUSELAH

Chrysostom,
it's time to toast 'em!

THE UNCLEAN

Chrysostom can go to Hell! He
and his toasts aren't any good
to a man with an empty belly!

METHUSELAH

Patience, brethren!
We'll stuff you with food
right away.

(He leads THE UNCLEAN *to a cloud table on which cloud milk and cloud bread have been set out.)*

CARPENTER

I'm worn out from walking.
Couldn't I have some sort of a chair?

METHUSELAH

I'm sorry.
In Heaven we have none.

CARPENTER *(pointing to the* MINER*)*

You might at least take pity on
our miracle-worker over there —
the one with the stoop.

MINER

Don't start to swear.
The main thing now is to recoup
our lost strength.

(THE UNCLEAN *grab at the bowls of cloud milk and hunks of cloud bread. Their initial amazement is followed by indignation, and they fling away the props.)*

METHUSELAH

Did you taste it?

CARPENTER *(menacingly)*

We tasted it, all right!
Don't you have something more material?

METHUSELAH

Should entities purely aerial
wallow in wine?

THE UNCLEAN

Down on earth, people humbly resign
themselves to death, hoping to see *you* –
you swine!
If they only knew
what lies ahead. Or rather, what *doesn't.*
Down there, paradises like yours
are a dime a dozen!

METHUSELAH *(pointing at the saint at whom the* BLACKSMITH *has been yelling)*

Don't yell at him – it's boorish.
He ranks among the seraphim.

FISHERMAN

Don't worry about taking care of him.
Just tell him to cook us up some borsch.

THE UNCLEAN

We never thought it would be like this!

HUNTER

It's a rat hole – that's what it is!

TRUCK DRIVER

And not at all like Heaven should be!

SHOEMAKER

Well, buddies, we wanted to go
to Heaven – and here we are!

SERVANT

It's a miserable dump, is what I say!

FARMHAND

So all you do is just sit here, eh?

ONE OF THE ANGELS

Why, no.
We sometimes go down to earth
to visit righteous sisters or brethren,
and then return,
having poured out our holy oil there.

SERVANT

What about the wear and tear
on your feathers
from rubbing against the clouds?
How silly! You'd do better
to get yourselves an elevator.

SECOND ANGEL

And besides, on the clouds we embroider
the letters J. C. –
the initials of our Savior.

SERVANT

You'd be better off chewing sunflower seeds,
you hicks!

FARMHAND

They should come visit me
down on earth. I'd fix
those bums so they'd never be lazy again!
At home, people sing:
"Down with the tyrants! Throw off your chains!"[1]

[*To the* DWELLERS IN PARADISE]

And they'll show you a thing
or two, too,
no matter how lofty you be.

SEAMSTRESS

It's just like in Petersburg: full
of people, and every last edible
eaten up!

THE UNCLEAN

This place is so dull!
So boring! Ugh!

METHUSELAH

What's to be done? It's the approved
way of doing things here. Naturally,
there is much that must still be improved.

INTELLECTUAL *(looking first at* TOLSTOY, *then at* ROUSSEAU; *he addresses the latter)*

I can't take my eyes off the two of you –
you and Leo Tolstoy.
How familiar your faces are to me!
Aren't you Jean-Jacques Rousseau?
Oh!
Permit me to tell you of the great joy
that is shaking my soul with its impact.
Was it you who wrote about liberty, equality,
 and fraternity?
Was it you who wrote *The Social Contract?*
Well, glory be!
Since ever so long ago,
I've known all your works by heart – and that's a fact!
Allow me to proffer
my compliments.
More than anything else in this world, I love reading
 an author
of liberal sentiments!
I'm not going anywhere.
I'm staying right here.
Let those uncouth Unclean go their way.
I *must* have a word with you, however briefly.
In your *Social Contract,* you say –

FARMHAND

How do we get out of this place?

METHUSELAH

Ask Gabriel.

FARMHAND

Which one is he?
They all look the same to me.

METHUSELAH *(proudly, stroking his beard)*

Don't say things like that!
There *are* distinctions.

It matters, for instance,
if one's beard be long.

THE UNCLEAN

What's to talk about? Let's wreck the joint!
This is one institution
where we don't belong.

COMPROMISER

Hush! Hush!
Comrades! Come!
Forget your quarrels, and agree!
Does it really matter what class I'm from?
(To the ANGELS)
Just look at them!
What husky chaps!
If I were in your shoes, I'd be
delighted at that.
The best part of society
is the proletariat!
[*To* THE UNCLEAN]
And you're a fine lot!
(Gesturing toward METHUSELAH)
Just consider the high rank he's got!
He's no Wrangel.[2]
He's an angel!

METHUSELAH

Agree with *them?*
God forfend!

BLACKSMITH

You think you're so bright!
I'll agree you, all right!
(They wallop him.)

COMPROMISER *(weeping)*

You try to be nice,
and it turns out nasty:
another bilateral castigation!
Oof!
One more attempt at conciliation,
and I'll give up the ghost!

FARMHAND

To the Promised Land!

Seek it somewhere beyond
Paradise! With our seven-league strides
we'll plow up Paradise!

ALL *(in chorus)*

We'll find it! If worse comes to worse,
we'll plow up the whole universe!

METHUSELAH *(looking at the havoc being wrought by* THE UNCLEAN *on Paradise; wails in a pathetic voice)*

Help! Police!
Catch them!
Arrest them!
May Almighty God strike them down with lightning!

(To the accompaniment of a terrifying peal of thunder, JEHOVAH *himself appears with a handful of thunderbolts.)*

JEHOVAH

With my thunderbolts, I'll strike you dead!

SOLDIER *(reproachfully)*

They're just like kids
who've tattled to Mama.

(Seeing a fracas of unprecedented proportions in the making, the COMPROMISER, *his face twisted up, begins to squeal.)*

COMPROMISER

Oof!
Jehovah himself!
I tremble!
I fall flat to the ground!
My knees buckle under me!

(To THE UNCLEAN*)*

Come to your senses!
Agree!
Are you mad?
Do you realize
you're opposing our gracious Lord?

JEHOVAH *(shaking his fist at the* COMPROMISER*)*

If I weren't He,
I'd show you a real compromise!

BLACKSMITH

Do you think we workers

could ever agree
with God? Your pacifist policy
will cost you dear!

COMPROMISER *(tearfully, but with respect)*

I greatly fear
my convictions are fading.
How you can hit!
A bit more conciliating,
and I'll lose my Menshevik spit
and polish.

LOCOMOTIVE ENGINEER *(pointing at* JEHOVAH, *who is brandishing his thunderbolts but is reluctant to use them for fear of hitting* METHUSELAH *and his band of angels)*

We must snatch away God's thunderbolts.
Take 'em!
We can use all those volts
for electrification.
Why waste peals of thunder on empty air?

(They throw themselves at JEHOVAH *and snatch his thunderbolts.)*

JEHOVAH *(sadly)*

They've plucked me bare!
Not a tuft of fuzz or a feather!

METHUSELAH

What can we use, now, to punish sinners?
We'll be forced out of business altogether.

(THE UNCLEAN, *carrying the thunderbolts, move upward.)*

BLACKSMITH

Dawn is breaking at last!
Onward –
beyond Paradise!
There we'll break our fast. . . .

(But when they have climbed up through the fragments and reached the summit, the SEAMSTRESS *interrupts the* BLACKSMITH.)

SEAMSTRESS

But can dawn nourish hungry men?

LAUNDRESS *(wearily)*

We break, we break, we break

the clouds.
Isn't it time we got past them?
How long till our weary bodies are bathed
in the freshness of May?

OTHER VOICES

Where to?
Won't we land in another Hell?
We've been duped –
and duped well.
And what comes next?
The farther we go, the worse it gets.
(After reflection)
Chimney sweep, go out ahead and scout!
(From the darkness of the fragments of Paradise, a new scene emerges. The COMPROMISER, *pensive, lags behind* THE UNCLEAN, *who keep going forward.)*

COMPROMISER

They've gone through Hell,
they've gone through Paradise,
and they're still going.
But wouldn't it be wise,
for me at least, to turn back?
They're a good bunch, those angels –
chaps worth knowing.
And they do seem to have a knack
for compromise.
(Waves after THE UNCLEAN *as they move off.)*
Let them go on, if that's the way they feel!
But I'll return
to Tolstoy. He's a big wheel!
And from him I'll learn
nonresistance to evil.

CURTAIN

ACT V

[*Land of Chaos*]

BLACKSMITH

Hey!
Why have you stopped?
Get a move on!

LAMPLIGHTER

We can't get. The mountains
have made our route impassable.
To travel a road like this is impossible.

SEAMSTRESS

How much rubbish has piled up
in three years' time!
(They look around at the fragments.)
Look – a piece of the ark!

SOLDIER

The remains
of the Negus of Abyssinia.

SHOEMAKER

A small chunk of Paradise.

FARMHAND

A cracked pot from Hell.

LAMPLIGHTER

What's to be done?
We can't go on,
and there's no place here to sit down.

BLACKSMITH

What's to be done? What's to be done?
We must clear away all this junk!

FARMHAND

No need for deliberation.

Let's get ourselves organized
and set to work!

SOLDIER *(with an air of self-importance)*

There is organization and organization.
The first matter we must take up
is planning correct policy.
An organizational shake-up
is called for, it seems to me.[1]

MINER *(annoyed)*

Now aren't you the clever chap!
Your shake-up is so much claptrap!
Appointed officials are what we need.

LAUNDRESS *(sarcastically)*

Appointed officials indeed!
We need buffers.[2]

(THE UNCLEAN *crowd together, arguing hotly.)*

ESKIMO HUNTER

To my mind,
none of these things agree
with Marxist dogma and form.
I take my stand
for a totally different platform.
I'm for saving the motherland
of the toiling Russians
by breaking the bonds of famine and poverty.

FARMHAND *(losing all hope)*

More discussion!

BLACKSMITH *(separating the belligerents)*

Comrades, please!
Cut it out!
This isn't a trade-union congress.

LOCOMOTIVE ENGINEER

Buffers? That miss is as good as a mile!
The laundress
has her own buffers under her dress,
but our locomotives don't even have wheels,
to say nothing of being bufferless.

BLACKSMITH

We drown in talk,
and can't see the ford.

On across the newspaper bilge,
and to work!
Forward!
Why drivel
a river of words?
Swing the pick!
Dig in with the shovel!

ALL *(in chorus, as they shovel away the debris)*

Now, then!
Swing once,
and swing again!
Why bother counting?
Strike once,
and once again, swing!

COMPROMISER *(sticking his head out from a cloud labeled "Berlin")*

Oh, oh, oh!
Comrades, stop working!
You yourselves know
I wouldn't give worthless advice.
From my foreign Paradise,
I can see everything.
Stop working, all you nice
people! Absolutely
nothing will come of it.
Agree with me –

BLACKSMITH

You stuck out your snout,
now look out!
Or my hammer will accidentally
give you a clout
on the forehead!

COMPROMISER

Wups!

(He immediately closes the cloud.)

MINER *(pausing, his pickax raised)*

Comrades,
listen!
I hear some kind of crying!
Somebody is being crushed

by the fragments,
and is dying!
Come! Rush
to his aid!
Dig hard!

(Hearing this, all dig with tenfold strength. From the clouds appear a LOCOMOTIVE *and a* STEAMSHIP.*)*

LOCOMOTIVE

Ai!
Hark to the locomotive's groan!
Don't let me die!
I can't get up a head
of steam.
Give me black bread
from the Don.[3]
Give me some food.
Hurry!

LOCOMOTIVE ENGINEER

Forget about death,
my friend. Don't worry.
We'll wrest coal from the bowels of the earth.
We'll conduct you to a new track.

STEAMSHIP

Alack! Alack! Alack!
Let me slake
my thirst at the sources of rivers!
I've got holes in either side, Doc!
Put me in dry dock!
Give me oil from Baku!
Ooh, ooh, ooh, ooh!

MINER

Hey, comrades,
follow me!
Why stand there with folded hands?
After the coal
beneath the earth's crust!
After the oil!
We must not let the petroliferous
sands

get away from us!

ALL *(in chorus)*

Lift your mattock, light as down!
Swing your pick with all your might!
Drive your drill into the ground!
Be a Stakhanovite!

CHAOS

Back!
Why do your hammers ring?
Back! Who is it challenging
me – Chaos?
I rule here as Queen –
Queen Chaos.
Your locomotives I gobble down.
I devour machines.
When I breathe,
I blow away factories like down.
When I breathe,
I blow away plants like fluff.
One look from me is enough
to make a train stop.
When I gnaw,
railroads are gobbled up.
And the city writhes in hunger
and cold;
and the country dies of cold
and hunger.
Back!
I hate cheerful labor.
Back!
Come, my host of self-seekers and loafers!
Come, loyal army of speculators!

(The "troops" of CHAOS *gather around her.)*

ALL *(in chorus)*

Back!
Why do your hammers ring?
Back!
Who is it challenging
her – Chaos?

CHAOS

Bow down! I'm Chaos – your Queen.
I'll make your throats tighten from hunger.

BLACKSMITH

Enough!
Let's clobber the Queen with a hammer!
To arms!

MINER *(advancing toward* CHAOS*)*

Let's seize the coal!
(Pointing to the PROFITEERS*)*
And these as well!
You've ridden the tops long enough.[4]
We'll herd all of you to work.

BLACKSMITH

Catch the self-seekers!
Away with the bums!
Everybody to work!
Work till you're numb!
(THE UNCLEAN *advance;* CHAOS' *"troops" retreat.)*

MINER *(cutting in under* CHAOS*)*

Must we bow our heads
before Chaos?
Comrades!
Cut under the trenches of the mines!

FARMHAND

Our trenches are furrows in the fields.

FARMHAND AND MINER

Our weapons are bread
and coal.

BLACKSMITH *(as* CHAOS *is slain; the last part of his speech is delivered over the corpse of* CHAOS*)*

Hurray!
They're running away!
Chaos is surrendering.
Just
one final blow remains to be struck. . . .
She has surrendered!
Enough!
(Pointing to the mine shaft)
Go on down!

The door into the future
is open.
Go on.
Drive shaft after shaft.
Sing out:
"This will be the last,
decisive battle."[5]

(They go into the mine shaft. Their voices die away in the distance.)

MINER *(wheeling out a hand truck loaded with coal)*
Here is the first Moscow batch.

LOCOMOTIVE
Thanks.
I'm glad.
I'll get my repairs.
Jack me up.

LOCOMOTIVE ENGINEER *(rolling out a barrel of crude oil)*
Here's the first gift
from Baku.

STEAMSHIP
I'm ready.
No more holes in my sides.

MINER *(with another truckload)*
And here's a gift
from the Don Basin.

LOCOMOTIVE
Thanks.
Now I'll work up steam.

LOCOMOTIVE ENGINEER *(with another barrel of oil)*
Here's another tank car of oil for you.

STEAMSHIP
Thanks.
Now my engines will go.

LOCOMOTIVE ENGINEER *(with another barrel of oil)*
And here's a gift from Ukhta.

MINER *(with another truckload)*
And this comes from the Urals.

STEAMSHIP AND LOCOMOTIVE
We're coming to life!
Hurray!

LOCOMOTIVE

My wheels are racing.

STEAMSHIP

I've come to life.
Now I'll rove the rivers.

(From the mine shafts THE UNCLEAN *rush forth and embrace one another.)*

LOCOMOTIVE ENGINEER

I'll help you.

MINER

And I'll help you.

BLACKSMITH

And I'll help both of you.

LAUNDRESS

Me, too.

SOLDIER

Extraordinary!

SEAMSTRESS

Beyond belief!

ESKIMO HUNTER

Fantastic news!

MINER

Look over there, beyond the last derrick!

MINER AND LOCOMOTIVE ENGINEER

There's something there!

MINER

I'm driving my last shaft.

LOCOMOTIVE ENGINEER

And this is the last
barrel I'll roll.

MINER

I hear,
from far, far away. . . .

LOCOMOTIVE ENGINEER

And I see something
far, far away – so far
that the eye can hardly make it out. . . .

MINER

I hear singing,
the rumbling of wheels,

the even breathing of factories. . . .

LOCOMOTIVE ENGINEER

I see the sun,
the early dawn,
and what must be a city.

SOLDIER

It looks as though we've won.
We seem to be
at the edge,
at the entrance
that leads into true Paradise.

LOCOMOTIVE

The locomotive is ready.

STEAMSHIP

The steamship is ready.

LOCOMOTIVE ENGINEER

Get yourselves ready to leave.
On those two
we'll rush into the future.

SOLDIER *(climbs into the* LOCOMOTIVE; *others follow him)*

The way is level,
smooth and clean.
Be the first one –
forward, engineer!
Over the waves!
Over the rails!
It is near –
that joy-filled home of the future,
earned by labor.
Eat up the distance,
breathing life
into machines. Only on them
can we make the stride
into the future.
Stroke after stroke!
Stride after stride!

ALL *(in chorus, repeating his words)*

Forward, breathing life
into all machines!

CURTAIN

ACT VI

The Promised Land. A huge gate. From behind its projecting corners can be glimpsed the streets and squares of an earthly city. Over the top of the gate one can see rainbows, roofs, and huge flowers. At the gate is a LOOKOUT, *who calls excitedly to* THE UNCLEAN *as they clamber up.*

MINER

This way, comrades!
This way!
Disembark for the landing!

(THE UNCLEAN *climb up and look over the gate with great astonishment.)*

MINER

Such marvels!

CARPENTER

But this is Ivanovo-Voznesensk![1]
Some marvels, I'll say!

SERVANT

I ask you: How can you trust those crooks?

BLACKSMITH

But this isn't Voznesensk,
believe me!
It's Marseilles!

SHOEMAKER

I think it's Shuya.[2]

TRUCK DRIVER

It's not Shuya at all –
it's Manchester.

LOCOMOTIVE ENGINEER

Aren't you ashamed to talk such bosh?

Manchester, indeed!
It's Moscow.
How come you're all blind?
See, there's Tverskaya Street,
and Sadovaya,
and the Theater
of the RSFSR.

FARMHAND

Moscow, Manchester, Shuya –
that's not the point.
The main thing is
that we're back on earth again,
in the same old hole.

ALL

The damned old world is round, all right!
It sure is round!

LAUNDRESS

It's the earth, but it's not the same any more.
For the earth, it doesn't stink
enough of slops.
Or so I think.

SERVANT

What's that I smell in the air –
like the fragrance of apricots?

SHOEMAKER

Apricots?
In Shuya?
But it's autumn, unless I miss my guess!

(They raise their heads, and a rainbow dazzles them.)

SOLDIER

Come on, Lamplighter!
You have a ladder.
Climb up
and take a look around.

LAMPLIGHTER *(climbs up, and then pauses, so stupefied he can only stammer)*

We're fools!
What fools we are!

SOLDIER

Well, out with it!
He's staring
like a goose that sees lightning.
Tell us,
you owl!

LAMPLIGHTER

I can't.
I'm tongue-tied.
Let me have a huge tongue
sixty miles long!
Let it be brighter and purer than the rays of the sun!
May it not hang like a rag!
May it give out the sound of the lyre!
May it be swung
by jewelers.
May words fly out of my mouth
like nightingales!
But then what?
Even then I couldn't begin to tell you!
Buildings a hundred stories high
cover the earth!
Graceful bridges are hung
between those buildings. And under them
an abundance of foods!
Heaps of things!
On the bridges, the tail ends of trains
disappear from sight!

ALL *(in chorus)*

Tail ends?

LAMPLIGHTER

Yes, the tail ends.
The lights stare
with electric eyes!
And motors of one million horsepower pour
their radiance
into those eyes!
The world sparkles and shines!

ALL *(in chorus)*

Shines?

LAMPLIGHTER

Yes, shines!

SOLDIER

You've worked yourselves.
Why is he surprised?

LOCOMOTIVE ENGINEER

Sure, we've worked. But still,
it's incredible
that work should produce
such a miracle!

FARMHAND

Enough balderdash!
You're some lecturer!
But nobody has ever yet made a silk purse
from a sow's ear.

LAMPLIGHTER

Stop your scolding!
This
is electrification!

ALL *(in chorus)*

Electrification?

LAMPLIGHTER

Yes,
electrification.
Plugs stuck into enormous sockets.

LOCOMOTIVE ENGINEER

Miracles!
No scientists would believe them!

LAMPLIGHTER

There goes an electric tractor!
An electric seeder!
An electric thrasher!
In one second
the bread
is already baked!

ALL *(in chorus)*

Baked?

LAMPLIGHTER

Yes,
baked.

BAKER

But the boss who looks like a bulldog pup,
and the boss's wife, all gussied up –
do they still stroll around the city,
making the sidewalks unpretty?

LAMPLIGHTER

No,
from here I can see no one.
I've noticed nothing of the kind.
There goes a sugar loaf!
Two more!

SEAMSTRESS

Sugar?
Did you hear that?
What can I do?
Just before the flood,
I lost my ration card.

ALL *(in chorus)*

Tell us in greater detail what you see.

LAMPLIGHTER

All sorts of victuals
and things
are walking around.
Each one has a hand,
each one has a foot.
The factories are all festooned
with banners.
Mile upon mile.
Wherever the hundred-legged worm
of my gaze turns,
I see,
decked in flowers,
the joiner's bench
and the lathe
standing idle.

THE UNCLEAN *(with anxiety)*

Standing?
Idle?
And here we are,
getting in trim via verbal athletics!

We may have rain
that will rust the machines!
Break in!
Shout!
Hey!
Who's there?

LAMPLIGHTER *(sliding down)*

They're coming!

ALL

Who?

LAMPLIGHTER

The Things.

(The gate flies open, and the city is revealed. What a city! The lattice-like forms of transparent factories and apartment buildings tower up toward the sky. Trains, streetcars, and automobiles stand wrapped in rainbows. In the center is a garden of stars and moons, surmounted by the radiant crown of the sun. From the showcases the best THINGS *come forth and, with the Hammer and Sickle at their head, advance to the gate to proffer bread and salt.*[3] THE UNCLEAN *are huddled together, stupefied.)*

THE UNCLEAN

Oh-oh-oh-oh!

THINGS

Ha, ha, ha, ha!

FARMHAND

Who are you?
And whose?

THINGS

What do you mean, "whose"?

FARMHAND

I mean, what is your master's name?

THINGS

We don't have any masters.
We belong to no one.
We're delegates.
The Hammer and Sickle –

the republic's seal —
greet you.

FARMHAND

But who's the bread for?
And the salt?
And the sugar loaf?
Are you greeting a governor, or what?

THINGS

No,
we're welcoming you.
All is yours.

LAUNDRESS

No more lies!
We're not little children.
You must be
black-market merchandise.
Probably
there's a whole horde of profiteers
behind all this.

THINGS

Not a single one!
Look and see!

SERVANT

I see what's going on!
You'll be held in reserve
by the Local Committee on Food Supplies,
and a year from now, they'll serve
you out to us, one spoonful at a time.

THINGS

We're not being stored anywhere.
Take a bushel apiece, if you like.

FISHERMAN

We must be asleep!
This must be a dream!

SEAMSTRESS

Once, I remember,
I sat
in the peanut gallery.
On stage was a ball.
La Traviata.

A banquet.
I went out,
and real life seemed so bitter then: all
mud,
and puddles.

THINGS

But from now on such things won't vanish.
This is the earth.

BLACKSMITH

Stop trying to fool us!
This isn't the earth!
The earth is dirt,
The earth is night.
On earth you work and earn your pay,
then the moment your back is turned,
some fat fellow comes along and takes away
what you've earned.

LAUNDRESS *(pointing at the bread)*

It calls,
but it
will bite,
I'll bet.
I'll wager a hundred thousand rubles
that it has a hundred thousand teeth
for every fifty loaves.

LOCOMOTIVE ENGINEER [*pointing to the* MACHINES]

And they're the same! . . .
Here they come!
They trot along as nice
and quiet as mice.
But they've mangled us often enough!
[*To the* MACHINES]
You'd just love to grow teeth
to use on the workers.

MACHINES

Forgive us, workman!
Workman, forgive!
You made us live:
mined the ore, smelted it,
and forged us.

But they seized us,
enslaved us.
"Run, machine!
Run, clumsy thing!"
Without ever stopping,
untiringly,
we creatures of steel
were ordered to carry the fat ones,
    running on tires,
were ordered to work in their factories.
Shaft on shaft,
for ages our flywheels
and driving belts tore you apart.
Shout, you motors!
A great joy is ours!
The fat ones are beaten.
From now on, we're free!
Roar in the factories, driving the wheels.
Turn round and round on the railroad lines.
Workers, from this day on,
we'll shine for you in the darkest night,
we'll make the world spin like a merry-go-round.

THINGS

And we're the auxiliary tools.
We're hammers, needles, saws, and tongs.
As soon as the first yellow streak of dawn
showed in the sky,
you used to go off to the factory,
stooped under our weight.
But now you've cleaned up on the gang
of bosses,
we fashion and forge everything for you.
To you, whose back broke beneath our weight,
we surrender today.
In the great blacksmith shop of the new Paradise,
raise high your sledgehammer, light as a toy.

EDIBLES

And we are the edibles, food and drink.
We've caused the workers untold sufferings.
Lacking bread, man lacks strength utterly;

lacking sugar, he knows nothing sweet.
Scarcely had we been produced
by men's labor, when *we* consumed *you* (not you, us)
through rubles inflated to gigantic sizes.
Opening wide the maw of high prices,
we barked like dogs from the windows of stores.
But you told the parasites, "Down from the seat
of power!"
From now on, bread and pastries are freed.
All that you used to gaze at, grinding your teeth,
is yours, now. Take it, slice it, and eat!

MACHINES, THINGS, AND EDIBLES *(in chorus)*

Take what is yours.
Take it!
Come and get
whatever you need to work with,
whatever you eat!
Come, take it!
Conqueror, come!

BLACKSMITH

I suppose we'll have to submit
an order for supplies.
But we don't have any with us.
We just came from Paradise,
and before that, from Hell.

THINGS

You won't need it.
No orders required at all.

FARMHAND

Our legs aren't razors —
we won't dull them, I'll bet.
Come, comrades, let's try it!
Let's go ahead!

(THE UNCLEAN *advance, and the* FARMHAND *touches the earth.)*

It's dear mother earth!
Our own native soil!

ALL

Let's sing.

Let's shout!
Let's say a prayer!

BAKER *(to the* CARPENTER*)*

That sugar –
I licked it.

CARPENTER

Well?

BAKER

It's sweet – oh, so sweet!

SEVERAL VOICES

Now joy will run wild!

FARMHAND *(getting tipsy)*

Comrade Things,
you know what?
Let's stop torturing Fate.
We'll manufacture you,
and you'll feed us. What say?
And if the boss tries to interfere,
we won't let him get away
alive.
Let's start to live.
OK?

ALL

Let's start to live!
Let's start to live!

MERCHANT *(having elbowed his way through the crowd; indignant, he hurries forward)*

I should say not!
You're going too far!
The concessionaire
is entitled to his share.

BLACKSMITH

Be off with you!
Your work is done.
You've made enough profit to buy baby's shoes!
We wanted to learn your know-how,
and we have.[4]
Now you can leave.

(Rejected, the MERCHANT *retires.* THE UNCLEAN *look avidly at the* THINGS.*)*

FARMHAND

I'd like a saw. I'm young,
and my hands have been idle too long.

SAW

Take me!

SEAMSTRESS

And I'd like a needle.

BLACKSMITH

My hands itch to work. Give me a hammer!

HAMMER

Take me, and hold me tight!

*(*THE UNCLEAN, *the* MACHINES, *and the* THINGS *form in a circle around the sunny garden.)*

LOCOMOTIVE ENGINEER *(to the* MACHINES)

I'd like to start you up.
You're sure you won't growl and come for me?

MACHINES

Don't worry!
Just turn the crank.

(The LOCOMOTIVE ENGINEER *turns the crank. Globes begin to glow, and wheels begin to turn.* THE UNCLEAN *look on, astonished and delighted.)*

LOCOMOTIVE ENGINEER

Never have I seen such light!
This isn't the earth,
it's a blazing meteorite
with a tail of trains.
Why did we bellow like oxen under the yoke?
We waited
and waited
and waited for years,
and never once did we notice
all these blessings right under our noses!
Why do folks go to museums, anyway?
All around us, treasures are heaped up high.
Is that the sky
or a piece of bright-colored cloth?
If this is the work of our own hands,
what door will not open before us?
We are the architects of earths,

the decorators
of planets. We're miracle-makers.
We'll tie rays of light
into bundles and use them as brooms
to sweep the clouds from the sky
with electricity.
We'll make the rivers of many worlds
splash honey. We'll pave the streets
on this earth with stars.
Dig!
Gouge!
Saw!
Bore!
All shout "Hurrah!
Hurray
for everything!"
Today,
these are only stage-prop doors,
but tomorrow, reality will replace
this theatrical trash.
We know this.
We believe in it.
Up here, spectator!
Up here, artist!
Poet!
Director!

(All the spectators mount the stage.)

ALL *(in chorus)*

Sun-worshipers in the temple
of this our world, let's show by example
how we can sing.
Form into choruses for a psalm
to the future!

(The COMPROMISER *appears from out of nowhere and stares with astonishment at the Commune. Realizing what is happening, he politely removes his hat.)*

COMPROMISER

No,
there's no place in Heaven for a man of energy.

I don't like the mugs on those fasting fellows.
Socialism is fated to be –
I've always said so.

(To THE UNCLEAN*)*

Comrades, don't shout so unpurposefully.
Singers' voices must always be made to agree
with each other.

(He goes off to one side and quietly leads the singing with his hand. The BLACKSMITH *politely shows him to the door.)*

THE UNCLEAN *(singing)*[5]

The great leviathan of labor
has stormed the prison of the past.
The world, which bore the curse of slavery,
has now been freed of it at last.
Oppression's chains were snapped and broken –
whirled off like dust clouds in a gale.
The Commune, once a fairy tale,
is here: its doors now stand wide open.

This is our victory chorale.
Let the whole universe sing!
Thanks to the "Internationale,"
mankind beholds a new spring.

We sought no aid from Him on high,
nor did the Devil lend a hand:
the workers went into the fray,
and seized the power in the land.
We've made the world one great Commune:
it's ringed round by the working class.
Just try to snatch it back again
from our determined, powerful grasp!

This is our victory chorale.
Let the whole universe sing!
Thanks to the "Internationale,"
mankind beholds a new spring.

The past will fade from memory.

The bourgeois have been wholly crushed.
Henceforth the earth belongs to us –
Labor's valiant soldiery.
Come from the field, the factory!
Come from the town, the village mall!
We hold the whole wide world in fee.
We who were naught, today are all.

This is our victory chorale.
Let the whole universe sing!
Thanks to the "Internationale,"
mankind beholds a new spring.

CURTAIN

1918–1921

THE BEDBUG

A Fantastic Comedy in Nine Scenes

Characters[1]

IVAN PRISYPKIN (alias PIERRE SKRIPKIN[2]), a former worker and former Party member, currently a fiancé

ZOYA BEREZKINA, a working girl

ELZEVIRA DAVIDOVNA RENAISSANCE,[3] a manicurist and cashier of a beauty parlor, engaged to PRISYPKIN

ROSALIA PAVLOVNA RENAISSANCE, her mother } hairdressers
DAVID OSIPOVICH RENAISSANCE, her father }

OLEG BAYAN,[4] an eccentric character, the owner of residential real estate

A POLICEMAN

A PROFESSOR

A ZOO DIRECTOR

A FIRE CHIEF

TWO GROOMS ATTENDANTS

[TWO BRIDESMAIDS]

[NUPTIAL GODFATHER]

[NUPTIAL GODMOTHER]

CHAIRMAN OF THE CITY COUNCIL

MASTER OF CEREMONIES

[AN INVENTOR]

A MACHINIST

[A CLEANING MAN]

AN OLD MAN } workers in an auditorium
A YOUNG MAN }

A SPEAKER

[PEDDLERS], REPORTERS, STUDENTS, FIREMEN, MEMBERS of the CITY COUNCIL, [DOCTORS], [CHORUS GIRLS], OLD PEOPLE, [MEN and WOMEN], a [GIRL], [a FOX-TROTTING COUPLE], [a BAREFOOTED YOUNG MAN], [BESPECTACLED YOUNG MAN], [YOUNG WORKER], MUSICIANS, SPECTATORS, ATTENDANTS (at the zoo), CHILDREN, HUNTERS

SCENE I

Center: huge revolving door of a department store. Sides: show windows full of merchandise. People coming in empty-handed and going out with packages. Peddlers selling their own merchandise walk through the aisles of the theatre.

MAN SELLING BUTTONS

Don't go and get married for lack of a button!
And don't get divorced for lack of the same!
Just squeeze with your thumb against your forefinger,
And your britches will never slide down, citizens!
Dutch buttons!
Mechanized –
They sew themselves on!
Six for twenty kopecks.
Step right up, gentlemen!

MAN SELLING DOLLS

Dancing dollies,
From the ballet and the Follies!
Outdoors or in,
The best toys there are!
They dance to the whim
Of the Commissar.

WOMAN SELLING APPLES

I don't have no pineapples
Or bananas today.
But I've got some fine apples.
Four kopecks apiece, lady. What do you say?

MAN SELLING WHETSTONES

Unbreakable
German
whetstones!

Just thirty
kopecks
each!
They'll sharpen
whatever
you want honed:
Your razor,
your knife,
or your tongue for a speech.
Try one!

MAN SELLING LAMPSHADES

Lampshades!
Any
color or size!
Red ones for passion,
and blue for tired eyes!
Equip yourselves, comrades!

MAN SELLING BALLOONS

Sausage balloons!
You can fly at your ease!
If General Nobile[1] had had one of these,
He wouldn't've come back from the Arctic so soon!
Here you are, citizens!

MAN SELLING SALTED HERRINGS

The best herrings
caught
by the State Fishing Trust!
With vodka and pancakes
they're strictly a must!

WOMAN SELLING LINGERIE

Fur-lined brassieres!
Fur-lined brassieres!

MAN SELLING GLUE

All over the world,
from Murmansk
to Hoboken,
People throw out
their crockery
as soon as it's broken.

But Excelsior glue
fixes anything
you've got,
From a statue
of Venus
to an old chamber pot.
Like some, lady?

WOMAN SELLING PERFUME

Coty perfume
by the quarter-ounce!
Coty perfume
by the quarter-ounce!

MAN SELLING BOOKS

What does a wife do when her husband's away? One hundred and five funny stories by the late Count Leo Nikolaievich Tolstoy! Only fifteen kopecks instead of a ruble twenty!

WOMAN SELLING LINGERIE

Fur-lined brassieres!
Fur-lined brassieres!

(Enter PRISYPKIN, ROSALIA PAVLOVNA, *and* OLEG BAYAN.)

WOMAN SELLING LINGERIE

Fur-lined –

PRISYPKIN *(excitedly)*

What aristocratic bonnets!

ROSALIA PAVLOVNA

Those aren't bonnets! They're –

PRISYPKIN

Do you think I'm blind? Just imagine! What if Elzevira and I have twins? That hat there would be for Dorothy, and the other for Lillian. I've already decided, you know, to give them aristocratic-cinematic names, like the Gish sisters. Yes, I can just see the two of them out for a stroll in those bonnets. Buy 'em, Rosalia Pavlovna! My home must be a horn of plenty!

BAYAN *(giggling)*

Go ahead and buy them! He's not really vulgar. It's just that he's from the new social class, so he sees things his own way. Just think what he's bringing into your family – an ancient, pure, proletarian origin and a union card! Yet you begrudge him a few rubles! His home must be a horn of plenty.

(ROSALIA PAVLOVNA, *sighing, makes the purchase.)*

BAYAN

I'll carry them. They're not heavy. Don't worry. There's no extra charge.

MAN SELLING DOLLS

Dancing dollies,
From the ballet and the Follies!

PRISYPKIN

My future children-to-be must be brought up in a refined atmosphere. Come on, Rosalia Pavlovna, buy one of those dolls!

ROSALIA PAVLOVNA

Comrade Prisypkin –

PRISYPKIN

Don't call me Comrade, Madame Citizen! Your daughter hasn't married into the proletariat yet!

ROSALIA PAVLOVNA

Well, Citizen Prisypkin, future Comrade, for that money fifteen men could have their beards shaved, not to mention the rest – mustaches and so on. Why not get an extra dozen bottles of beer for the wedding instead?

PRISYPKIN *(sternly)*

Rosalia Pavlovna, my home –

BAYAN

His home must be a horn of plenty. The beer must gush forth like a geyser – and the dancing, too – as if from a cornucopia.

(ROSALIA PAVLOVNA *buys.)*

BAYAN *(grabbing the packages)*

Don't worry! No extra charge.

MAN SELLING BUTTONS

Don't go and get married for lack of a button!
And don't get divorced for lack of the same!

PRISYPKIN

In our Red family there must be no petty bourgeois

way of life, and no trouserly squabbles. Go on! Buy some, Rosalia Pavlovna!

BAYAN

So long as you don't have a union card, you'd better not give him any trouble. He is the working class. Like lava from a volcano, he sweeps away everything in his path. Comrade Prisypkin's pants must be a horn of plenty.

(ROSALIA PAVLOVNA, *sighing, buys some buttons.*)

BAYAN

Allow me. I'll carry them. No extra charge.

MAN SELLING SALTED HERRINGS

The best herrings caught by the State Fishing Trust!
With any kind of vodka, they're strictly a must!

ROSALIA PAVLOVNA *(loudly, her mood brightening, elbowing everyone else aside)*

Herrings! That's more like it! Something we really need for the wedding. Yes, I'll get some of those, all right! Let me through, please! How much are those little herrings!

MAN SELLING HERRINGS

That salmon is two-sixty a kilo.

ROSALIA PAVLOVNA

What? Two-sixty for those overgrown tadpoles?

MAN SELLING HERRINGS

Come now, madame! Only two-sixty for that candidate for sturgeonship!

ROSALIA PAVLOVNA

Two-sixty for those marinated corset bones? Did you hear that, Comrade Skripkin?[2] Now I can see you people were right when you killed the Tsar and drove out the millionaires![3] Oh, these robbers! I'm going to the Soviet State *Socialized* Co-op for my herrings – and for my civil rights, too!

BAYAN

Let's wait here, Comrade Skripkin. Why should you get involved with these petty bourgeois elements and buy herrings via such argumentative procedure? For fifteen rubles and a bottle of vodka, I'll organize a wedding that'll suit you to a "*T*."

PRISYPKIN

Comrade Bayan, I'm against all this petty bourgeois way of life – canaries and all the rest of it. I'm a man with expansive needs. I'm interested in a clothes-closet with a mirror.

(ZOYA BEREZKINA *nearly bumps into them as they stand talking; amazed, she steps back and listens.)*

BAYAN

When your wedding cortege –

PRISYPKIN

What are you going on about – some kind of card game?

BAYAN

"Cortege," I said. In those pretty foreign languages, that's the name they use for a procession – especially a wedding procession.

PRISYPKIN

Well, isn't that something!

BAYAN

And so, when the cortege approaches, I'll recite the epithalamium of Hymen.

PRISYPKIN

What the devil are you talking about? What Himalayas?

BAYAN

Not "Himalayas." An epithalamium to the god Hymen. He was a god of love that the Greeks had. I mean the ancient, republican Greeks – not the low-down, cheap Greeks in power today.

PRISYPKIN

Comrade Bayan, for my money I demand a Red wedding with no gods. Get me?

BAYAN

Come now! Of course I understand you. Not only that, but by virtue of that powerful imagination with which, according to Plekhanov[4], all Marxists are endowed, I can visualize as through a prism your class-conscious, lofty, elegant, and rapturous wedding ceremony! The bride climbs out of her carriage. She's a Red[5] bride – red all over; all in a sweat, that is. She is holding the arm of another red individual, the bookkeeper Yerikalov, who is to give her away, and who happens to be fat, red, and apoplectic. You are brought in by red groomsmen; the table is heaped with red hams; and the wine bottles all have red seals on them.

PRISYPKIN *(enthusiastic)*

That's it! That's it!

BAYAN

The red guests all shout, "Bitter! Bitter! Make it sweet!"[6] And the red girl, already your spouse, puts her red, red lips to yours –

ZOYA *(losing control of herself, grabs both of them by the arms; they shake her off and brush off their sleeves)*

Vanya! What's going on? What is he jabbering about – this cuttlefish in a cravat? What wedding? Whose wedding?

BAYAN

The Red, working-class nuptials of Elzevira Davidovna Renaissance and –

PRISYPKIN

My dear, I've found another love
Who's daintier than you, I trow:
Her sweater clings to what's above,
Her skirt to everything below.[7]

ZOYA

Vanya! What about me? You mean you've loved me and left me just like a sailor?

PRISYPKIN *(holding her off with outstretched arm)*

We have parted, like ships on the sea –

ROSALIA PAVLOVNA *(rushing in from the shop, holding a herring above her head)*

Whales! Dolphins! *(To the* MAN SELLING HERRINGS*)* Just show me that snail! Let's compare! *(She compares the herrings; the peddler's are bigger. She wrings her hands.)* Longer by a tail's length? Then what did we struggle for, Citizen Skripkin? Why did we kill our Tsar and chase out the millionaires? Answer me that! This Soviet regime of yours will be the death of me yet! Longer by a tail's length – a whole tail's length!

BAYAN

My esteemed Rosalia Pavlovna, try comparing them at the other end. They're only bigger by a head. And why do you need the heads? You can't eat them anyway. You'll just cut them off and throw them away.

ROSALIA PAVLOVNA

Did you hear that? Did you hear what he said? Citizen Bayan, it's your head I'm going to cut off. Nobody would lose anything by that. But if I cut off the heads of these herrings, I'll lose ten kopecks to the kilo. Well, come on. Let's go home. I'll admit I need a union card in the family. But still, my daughter's in a good business, and that's nothing to sneeze at.

ZOYA

We were going to live together and work together! And now it's all off. . . .

PRISYPKIN

Citizen, our love has been liquidated! And if you interfere with my civic rights to freedom of feeling, I'll call the police.

(ZOYA, *crying, grabs him by the arm.* PRISYPKIN *shakes her off.* ROSALIA PAVLOVNA *comes between them, dropping her packages.)*

ROSALIA PAVLOVNA

What do you want, you slut? Why are you hanging on to my son-in-law?

ZOYA

He's mine!

ROSALIA PAVLOVNA

Aha! So she's pregnant! I'll pay her off, all right! I'll smash her ugly mug!

POLICEMAN

Citizens! Stop this disgraceful squabbling!

SCENE II

A dormitory for young workers and students. An INVENTOR *is laboring wheezily over a blueprint; a* BAREFOOTED YOUNG MAN *is wandering around; a* GIRL *is sitting on the edge of the bed; a* BESPECTACLED YOUNG MAN *has his nose buried in a book. When the door is opened, one can see a long corridor with doors along the sides and light bulbs at intervals overhead.*

BAREFOOTED YOUNG MAN *(yelling)*

Where are my shoes? Somebody's swiped them again. Do I have to check them at the baggage room at Kursk Station every night? Is that what I have to do?

CLEANING MAN

Prisypkin put 'em on to go see his she-camel. All the time he was getting into 'em, he kept swearing. And he said, "This is the last time! Tonight I shall appear in a new external aspect – one more suitable to my new social status."

BAREFOOTED YOUNG MAN

That swine!

YOUNG WORKER *(tidying up the room)*

The mess he leaves around the room these days is classier stuff than it used to be – more refined, sort of. Before, it was just empty beer bottles and fish tails. Now it's cologne bottles and neckties of all colors of the rainbow.

GIRL

Oh, stop your jabbering! The guy gets himself a new necktie, and you go on like he was Ramsay MacDonald.

BAREFOOTED YOUNG MAN

That's just what he is – a Ramsay MacDonald. It isn't the necktie that matters. The trouble is, he's tied to the tie, not the tie to him. He doesn't even think any more. He's afraid he might rumple his brains.

CLEANING MAN

He paints over the holes in his clothes with enamel. If he sees a hole in his sock, and he's in a hurry, he just dabs some ink over it while he's dressing.

BAREFOOTED YOUNG MAN

His feet are black even without the ink.

INVENTOR

But maybe they're not black in the places where the holes are. What he should do, he should switch socks.

CLEANING MAN

Brilliant! What an inventor! You'd better take out a patent before somebody steals your idea.

(As the CLEANING MAN *is wiping a desk with his dust rag, he knocks over a box, from which visiting cards spill out, fanwise. He bends down to pick them up, holds one up to the light, and begins to laugh so hard he can barely manage to signal the others to come over to look.)*

ALL *(reading, repeating after one another)*

Pierre Skripkin! Pierre Skripkin!

INVENTOR

That's the new name he's invented for himself. Just consider the name Prisypkin. What's a Prisypkin, anyway? What good is Prisypkin? What can you do with Prisypkin? Who needs Prisypkin? But Pierre Skripkin, now – that's not a name, it's a song of love.

GIRL *(dreamily)*

You're right! Pierre Skripkin is very elegant and distinguished. You others can go ahead and laugh. But for all you know, he may be carrying out a cultural revolution right in his own home.

BAREFOOTED YOUNG MAN

With that mug of his, he's even got Pushkin beat. Those sideburns hang down like hounds' tails. He doesn't even wash his face – he's afraid he might tousle them up.

GIRL

That German movie actor, Harry Piel – he has the same kind of "culture" growing all the way down both sides of his face.

INVENTOR

Prisypkin's culture is being developed by Oleg Bayan, his teacher in the hairy area of the curriculum.

BAREFOOTED YOUNG MAN

Yes, and what is there for his teacher's hair to grow on? He doesn't have a head – only a lot of curly fuzz. What do you think makes it grow like that? Maybe it's the humidity.

BESPECTACLED YOUNG MAN

You've got it all wrong about Bayan. He's a writer. I don't know what he's written, but he's famous! There were write-ups about him in *The Evening Moscow* three different times. They say he plagiarized from Apukhtin,[1] so Apukhtin got mad and challenged him in print. His answer was, "You're all crazy, and nothing you say is true. I stole those poems from Nadson."[2] They don't publish him any more, but he's still very famous. He gives lessons to young people. He teaches them singing, dancing, how to write poetry, and – well – how to borrow money.

YOUNG WORKER *(wielding a broom)*

Painting over the corns on his feet with enamel! That's not a thing for a worker to do!

> (A MACHINIST, *covered with grease, has entered during this speech; he washes his hands and turns around.)*

MACHINIST

Prisypkin? He's the farthest thing from a worker! He quit his job today. He's getting married – to a hairdresser's daughter. She's the cashier, and she's a manicurist besides. From now on he'll be getting his claws clipped by Mademoiselle Elzevira Renaissance.

INVENTOR

Elzevira? That's the name of a type face.

MACHINIST

I don't know about faces, but she has a body, that's for sure! Today, when he wanted the pay clerk to hurry up and give him his check, he showed him her picture.

What a dolly! What a pet!
Each breast weighs eighty pounds, I'll bet.

BAREFOOTED YOUNG MAN

He's got himself all fixed up!

GIRL

What's the matter? You jealous?

BAREFOOTED YOUNG MAN

Maybe I am. But when they make me a foreman, and I get some regular shoes, *I'll* start looking around for a nice little apartment, too.

MACHINIST

While you're at it, you'd better get yourself some curtains. You could open 'em when you wanted to take a look outside, and close 'em whenever you took a bribe. . . . Being off by yourself may be bad when you're working: a man likes company then. But when it comes to a tasty dish, you like to enjoy it in private, right? In the war, we had plenty of men who tried to get away from the trenches and find a soft spot. But we slapped them down. Well, what are you waiting for? Go on – get out!

BAREFOOTED YOUNG MAN

Don't worry, I will! But I'd like to know just who you think you are – Karl Liebknecht?[3] If a girl waved a flower at you from a window, I'll bet you'd go for it, too, you big hero!

MACHINIST

No, I'll never leave my post. You think I like these dirty rags and this stink? Well, I don't. But there're lots of us, remember, so there's just not enough businessmen's daughters to go around.[4] We'll put up buildings, and we'll move forward all at the same time – together. But we'll never crawl out of this trench with a white flag!

BAREFOOTED YOUNG MAN

Can't you talk about anything but trenches? Today isn't 1919. People want to live for themselves now.

MACHINIST

Well, isn't this place like a trench?

BAREFOOTED YOUNG MAN

Horseshit!

MACHINIST

Lice all over the place!

BAREFOOTED YOUNG MAN

Horseshit!

MACHINIST

But they're shooting with noiseless powder.[5]

BAREFOOTED YOUNG MAN

Horseshit!

MACHINIST

Just look at Prisypkin there. He's been wounded by a shot from the double-barreled eyes of a woman!

(Enter PRISYPKIN *and* BAYAN. *The former is wearing patent-leather shoes. From one outstretched hand he dangles by their laces a worn-out pair of shoes, which he tosses to the* BAREFOOTED YOUNG MAN. BAYAN *is loaded down with purchases. He comes between* PRISYPKIN *and the* MACHINIST, *who has started to dance a jig.)*

BAYAN

Comrade Skripkin, don't pay any attention to that vulgar dance. It will only corrupt the refined taste you have just begun to develop.

(The others in the dormitory turn their backs.)

MACHINIST

Oh, quit your bowing and scraping! You're liable to crack your noggin on the floor!

BAYAN

I understand how it is, Comrade Skripkin. With your tender soul, their vulgar company is hard to put up with – impossible, really. But try to keep your patience intact for just one more lesson. The first foxtrot after the wedding ceremony is a very important step in life. The impression it makes must stay with you for the rest of your days. All right now, try a few steps with an imaginary partner. . . . Why are you stamping your feet like that? You're not in a May Day parade!

PRISYPKIN

Comrade Bayan, I have to take off my shoes. In the first place, they pinch. And in the second place, they'll wear out.

BAYAN

That's it! That's the way! Tread softly, as if you were coming home from a beer joint on a moonlight night, in a dreamy and melancholy mood. That's right! But don't wiggle your behind like that! You're supposed to be leading a girl, not pushing a cart! That's better! . . . Where's your hand? Bring it up higher!

PRISYPKIN *(passing his hand over an imaginary shoulder)*

I can't keep my hand up in the air!

BAYAN

And now, comrade, you gently probe her defenses, locate her brassiere, and hook your thumb in it as if you wanted to rest it there. The feeling of sympathy is pleasant to the lady, and for you it's a relief – because now you can think about your other hand. . . . Why are you jiggling your shoulders? You're not doing the foxtrot – you're demonstrating the shimmy!

PRISYPKIN

No I'm not! It's just that – well, I was scratching myself.

BAYAN

But that just isn't done, Comrade Prisypkin! If any such emergency should occur while you're enraptured by the dance, just roll your eyes as though in a fit of jealousy, back up to the wall in the Spanish manner, and scratch yourself quickly on some statue or other. In the elegant society where you'll be moving, they always have lots of statues and vases around. Then when you've scratched your back, you screw up your face, get a flash in your eyes, and say, "I see what you're up to, tr-r-reacherous one! You're playing games with me! But. . . ." At which point you whirl her off in the dance again, as if you've begun to cool off and calm down.

PRISYPKIN

Like this?

BAYAN

Bravo! Very good! Comrade Prisypkin, you have real talent. What with bourgeois encirclement and the building of socialism in one country, you just don't have room to expand. Goat Alley is no place for you. You need a world revolution – a breakthrough to Europe. Once you've smashed the Chamberlains and Poincarés, you'll be a sensation at the Moulin Rouge and the Pantheon, too, with the beauty of your bodily movements! Just remember them. Hold it. That's excellent! . . . But I have to run along. I've got to keep an eye on those ushers. I'll give them one drink before the wedding, and not a drop more. Once they've done their job, they can drink right out of the bottle, for all I care. *Au revoir! (Shouting from the door as he leaves.)* Don't put on two ties together – especially if they're different colors! And for God's sake remember you can't wear a starched shirt outside your trousers!

(PRISYPKIN *tries on his new clothes.)*

YOUNG MAN

Vanka, why don't you drop all this silly business? How did you ever get to be such a stuffed shirt?

PRISYPKIN

None of your damned business, my esteemed comrade! What did I fight for, anyway? For a good life, that's what! And now it's all within my reach: a wife, a home, and real refinement. If I have to, I'll do my duty as well as the next man. Meanwhile:

He who has fought is well entitled
To rest beside the quiet stream.[6]

So there! And who knows? Maybe just by looking after my own comfort I can raise the standards of the whole working class!

MACHINIST

A warrior! Another Suvorov! Exactly!
I built it high, and I built it low –
That bridge to socialism, Oh!
But I grew weary ere 'twas done,
And I sat me down to rest my bones.

Now the grass grows high, and the sheep graze low,
On that bridge to socialism, Oh!
For I gave up my socialist dream
To rest beside the quiet stream.[7]

That's right, isn't it?

PRISYPKIN

To hell with you! Leave me alone with your crude propaganda verses! *(Sits down on the bed and begins to sing, with a guitar.)*

I recall an ancient house
That stood on Lunacharsky Street:
The stairs were broad and marvelous,
The windows elegant and neat.

(A shot. Everyone rushes to the door.)

YOUNG MAN *(from the doorway)*

Zoya Berezkina just shot herself! She'll catch hell for that at the next Party meeting!

VOICES

Help!
Help!
First aid!
First aid!

A VOICE *(on the telephone)*

First aid? Hurry! . . . What? A girl shot herself. In the breast. It went clear through. This is Goat Alley, Number 16.

(PRISYPKIN, *left alone, hurriedly gathers up his belongings.)*

MACHINIST

To think such a woman would shoot herself on account of you – you hairy-faced bastard! *(Grabs* PRISYPKIN *by the jacket and heaves him out the door, throwing his things after him.)*

CLEANING MAN *(enters on the run with a doctor, pulls* PRISYPKIN *to his feet, and gives him his hat, which has fallen off)*

Well, buddy, I must say you're breaking off from your class with a bang![8]

PRISYPKIN *(turns on his heel and yells)*

Cabby! Seventeen Lunacharsky Street – with my bags!

SCENE III

A large room serving as a combination beauty parlor and barbershop. Mirrored walls, before which paper flowers are arranged. Bottles on the washstands. On the left, upstage, a grand piano with open jaws. On the right, a stove whose pipe goes twisting and winding through the room. In the center, a round banquet table. Seated at the table are PIERRE SKRIPKIN, ELZEVIRA RENAISSANCE, TWO BRIDESMAIDS *and* TWO GROOM'S ATTENDANTS, "MAMA" *and* "PAPA" RENAISSANCE, NUPTIAL GODFATHER *(a bookkeeper)*, NUPTIAL GODMOTHER *(his wife)*. OLEG BAYAN *is seated center stage, with his back to the audience.*

ELZEVIRA

Shall we begin, Skripochka?

SKRIPKIN

Just a minute.

(A pause)

ELZEVIRA

Skripochka darling, shall we begin?

SKRIPKIN

I said, "Just a minute." I want to get married in an organized manner and in the presence of distinguished guests – especially in the presence of the secretary of our factory committee, the esteemed Comrade Lassalchenko. . . . So there!

GUEST *(running in)*

Esteemed bride and groom! Please be so magnanimous as to forgive my delay. I have been empowered by our esteemed leader, Comrade Lassalchenko, to convey his nuptial congratulations to you. "Tomorrow," he says, I'd even be willing to go to a church for the wedding. But today," he says, "there's a Party meeting, and whether I like it or not, I have to go to the Party cell." And so, as they say, let us proceed to current business.

PRISYPKIN

I hereby declare the wedding open.

ROSALIA PAVLOVNA

Comrades and messieurs! Please start eating! Where could you find pigs like these nowadays? I bought this ham three years ago in case of a war with Greece, or maybe with Poland. But there's still no war, and the ham is going bad. Eat, messieurs!

ALL *(raising their glasses)*

Bitter! Bitter! Make it sweet!

*(*ELZEVIRA *and* SKRIPKIN *kiss.)*

Bitter! *Bi-i-i-t—ter!*

*(*ELZEVIRA *drapes herself around* SKRIPKIN*'s neck. He kisses her sedately, with an air of working-class dignity.)*

NUPTIAL GODFATHER

Give us some Beethoven! Some Shakespeare! Let's have a show! Otherwise, what's the use of always celebrating those anniversaries?

(The grand piano is dragged stage center.)

VOICES

The sides! Take hold of the sides! Oh, just look at the teeth it has! Makes you want to smash 'em!

PRISYPKIN

Don't trample on the legs of my piano!

BAYAN *(stands up, weaves from side to side, and spills some of his drink)*

I am happy, most happy, to witness the elegant conclusion, at this given interval of time, of the all-out fight that Comrade Skripkin has waged all along the way. True enough, somewhere along the way he lost his Party card. But on the other hand, he did acquire many government lottery tickets. We have succeeded in harmonizing and coordinating the class contradictions and other conflicts between the bride and groom. And he who is armed with the Marxist view cannot fail to see in this fact, as in a drop of water, so to speak, the future happiness of mankind – that which the common people call socialism.

ALL

Bitter! Bitter!

(ELZEVIRA *and* SKRIPKIN *kiss.*)

BAYAN

What great strides we are making in our forward march along the path of family construction! At the battle of Perekop,[1] when all of us lay dying – and when many even did – could we have imagined that these roses would bloom and waft their fragrance to us so soon, at this given interval of time? When we were groaning under the yoke of autocracy, could even our great teachers, Marx and Engels, have conjecturally dreamed – or even dreamily conjectured – that someday we would join together by the bonds of Hymen these two: Labor, humble but great; and Capital, dethroned yet still enchanting.

ALL

Bitter! Bitter!

BAYAN

Esteemed comrades! Beauty is the propulsive force of progress! As an ordinary worker, with my former name of Bochkin, what would I have amounted to? Just Bochkin, that's all. And as Bochkin, what could I have done? Just bellowed, that's all! But as Oleg Bayan I can do anything. For instance:

I'm Oleg the poet –
Sloppy drunk, and I know it.

And so now I'm Oleg Bayan, and as a fully privileged member of society I enjoy all the blessings of culture. And I swear that – Well, no, I can't swear here, but at least I can talk like an ancient Greek:

Please, Madame Skripkin – Elzevir –
Pass me the fish now, would you, dear?

And then maybe the whole nation will reply, like so many troubadours:

Oleg, your whistle is not yet
Elegantly and thoroughly wet.
So please drink from this glass of ale,
And gobble up this herring's tail.

ALL

Bravo! Hurrah! Bitter! Bitter!

BAYAN

Beauty is the mother –

FIRST GROOM'S ATTENDANT *(leaps to his feet, menacingly)*

"Mother – ?" Who said "Mother – ?" You'd better watch your language in the presence of newlyweds.

(The GROOM'S ATTENDANT *is hauled offstage.)*

ALL

Give us some Beethoven! Let's have a folk dance!

*(*BAYAN *is dragged to the piano.)*

BAYAN

The streetcar drew up to the Registry Hall,
Where a Red wedding was in progress. . . .

ALL *(in chorus)*

The groom was wearing his coveralls,
With a union card in his left front pocket.

NUPTIAL GODFATHER

I get it! I get the whole idea! It means:
May you fare well, Oleg Bayankin,
Little curly-headed lambkin. . . .

PAPA RENAISSANCE *(holding his fork, leans toward the* NUPTIAL GODMOTHER)

No, madame, no! Today, after the Revolution, there's no such thing as genuine curls. Here's how you make a *chignon gaufré:* you take the curling iron *(Picks up his fork and turns it),* heat it over a low flame – *à l'étoile (Sticks his fork into the flame from the stove)* – and then whip up a kind of *soufflé* of hair on top of the head.

NUPTIAL GODMOTHER

You are insulting my honor as a mother and as a girl! Lay off it, you son of a bitch!

SECOND GROOM'S ATTENDANT

Who said "son of a bitch?" You'd better watch your language in the presence of newlyweds!

(The NUPTIAL GODFATHER *separates them, still singing and trying to crank the handle of the cash register, dancing around with it as if it were a barrel organ.)*

ELZEVIRA *(to* BAYAN)

Oh, please play for us! Play that waltz, "Makarov's Lament for Vera Kholodnaya."[2] Oh, it's so *charmant!* A real *petite histoire!*

SECOND GROOM'S ATTENDANT *(armed with a guitar)*

Who said *"pissoir?"* You'd better watch –

(BAYAN *separates them and pounces on the piano keyboard.)*

(Watching him closely, with a threatening look) Why are you playing just on the black keys? You think only half of the keys are good enough for the proletariat? It's only for the bourgeoisie that you play on all of them?

BAYAN

What do you mean, citizen? I'm playing mostly on the white keys!

SECOND GROOM'S ATTENDANT

So now it turns out that the white keys are best? Play on both!

BAYAN

But I *am* playing on both!

SECOND GROOM'S ATTENDANT

So you go along with the Whites? You're a compromiser?

BAYAN

But, comrade . . . the thing is, I'm playing in C major A simple tone –

SECOND GROOM'S ATTENDANT

Who said "simpleton?" And in front of the newlyweds, too! Take that! *(Hits* BAYAN *on the back of the neck with a guitar.)*

(PAPA RENAISSANCE *twists his fork in the* NUPTIAL GRANDMOTHER's *hair.* PRISYPKIN *pulls the* NUPTIAL GODFATHER *away from his wife.)*

PRISYPKIN

What's the big idea, shoving a herring into my wife's bosom? That's a bosom, not a flower bed! And that's not a chrysanthemum – it's a herring!

SECOND GROOM'S ATTENDANT

And did you serve us salmon? *Did you*? So what are you yelling about, eh?

(In the general melee the bride in her gossamer dress is pushed onto the stove, and the stove overturns. Flames. Smoke.)

VOICES

We're on fire!
Who said, "We're on fire?"
Fire!
Salmon! . . .
The streetcars drove off from the Registry
Hall. . . .

SCENE IV

In the total darkness of the night, a fireman's helmet gleams, reflecting the light from a nearby fire. The FIRE CHIEF *alone remains continuously on stage, while various* FIREMEN *enter, report to him, then leave.*

FIRST FIREMAN

We can't control it, Comrade Chief! It was two hours before anybody called us – the drunken swine! Now it's burning like a powder magazine. *(Leaves.)*

FIRE CHIEF

How could it help burning? All cobwebs and liquor!

SECOND FIREMAN

It's beginning to die down. The water's turning to icicles while it's still in the air. The cellar is flooded and frozen over – like a skating rink, only smoother. *(Leaves.)*

FIRE CHIEF

Have you found any bodies?

THIRD FIREMAN

We've loaded up one with his dome all smashed in. Must have been hit by a collapsing beam. Sent him straight to the morgue. *(Leaves.)*

FOURTH FIREMAN

We just loaded up another – a charred body of undetermined sex with a fork stuck in its head.

FIRST FIREMAN

One former female found under the stove with a wire crown on the back of the skull.

THIRD FIREMAN

One unidentified corpse of prewar physique with a cash register in his hands. He must have been a burglar.

SECOND FIREMAN

No survivors. . . . One body missing. In view of the fact that it hasn't been found, I assume it was burned up entirely.

FIRST FIREMAN

Such fireworks! Just like a theater – only all the actors have been burned up!

THIRD FIREMAN

They were driven from the marriage –
With a Red Cross on the carriage.

(A bugler summons the FIREMEN. *They form ranks, and march down the aisle of the theater, reciting:)*

Citizens and comrades,
vodka is poisonous!
Drunkards
are setting
the republic aflame!
Beware of fireplaces,
beware of primuses –
If your house catches fire,
you may well do the same!
Also,
fires often start
when people doze off,
So never
read Nadson
or Alex Zharov![1]

SCENE V

[Fifty years later]

A huge auditorium, in the form of an amphitheater. In lieu of people and their voices, radio loudspeakers; beside each with an arm that can move up and down, as though signaling from an automobile window. Above each loudspeaker, colored light bulbs. Just below the ceiling, a movie screen. In the middle of the auditorium, a speakers' rostrum with a microphone; along its sides, control panels for sound and light. Two technicians — an OLD MAN *and a* YOUNG MAN *— are tinkering around in the darkened auditorium.*

OLD MAN *(dusting the loudspeakers with a worn-out feather duster)*

They're voting on something important today. Better check the voting equipment for the farming regions and give it an oiling. Something was wrong with it last time. The voices sounded squeaky.

YOUNG MAN

The farming regions? All right. I'll oil the central sections. And I'll clean out the throat of the Smolensk units. They were sounding hoarse again last week. And I have to tighten up the arms for the Moscow office personnel. They're a bit out of whack — the right one keeps tangling with the left.

OLD MAN

The plants in the Urals are ready. We'll cut in the Kursk steel mills. They've installed a new unit out there for sixty-two thousand voters at the second group of Zaporozhe power plants. It works fine — never any trouble.

YOUNG MAN

Do you still remember how it was in the old days? Must have been pretty silly, uh?

OLD MAN

My mother took me to a meeting once – carried me in her arms. Not many people there – maybe a thousand. They just sat there like so many idlers, listening. It was a very important motion, and it passed by just one vote. My mother was against it, but she couldn't raise her arm to vote because of me.

YOUNG MAN

Yes, well, things were pretty primitive then.

OLD MAN

In those days, even equipment like this wouldn't have worked. The thing was, a man had to get his hand up *first* in order to be noticed. So he'd stick it right in the chairman's face – even shove both hands up against his nose. A voter like that – well, it's too bad he wasn't the ancient goddess Isis. Then he could have voted with twelve hands.

And then, you know, a lot of people just ducked out of voting. They used to tell about one man who sat out a whole meeting – and a very important one, too – in the men's room. He was too scared to vote. So he just sat there thinking how to keep his nose clean.

YOUNG MAN

And did he?

OLD MAN

Oh, yes! But they assigned him to a new job – a new specialty. Seeing how much he liked the men's room, they made him head man there in charge of the soap and towels. . . . Everything ready?

YOUNG MAN

Ready!

(They hurry down to the control panels. The SPEAKER, *a bearded man with glasses, flings open the door and walks straight to the rostrum. With his back to the auditorium, he raises both hands.)*

SPEAKER

Switch in all regions of the Federation simultaneously!

OLD MAN and YOUNG MAN

They're cut in!

(Simultaneously, all of the red, green, and blue bulbs light up.)

SPEAKER

Hello! Hello! This is the president of the Institute of Human Resurrection, speaking! The question to be voted on has already been communicated by circular telegram, and discussed. It is simple and clear. On the site of the former city of Tambov, at the intersection of Sixty-second Street and Seventeenth Avenue, a construction crew excavating a foundation discovered an ice-filled cellar buried under seven meters of earth. Clearly visible through the ice was a frozen human figure. The Institute considers it possible to resurrect this individual, who was frozen fifty years ago.

Let us now vote to adjust the differences of opinion. The Institute considers that the life of every worker must be utilized to the last second.

X-rays have revealed calluses on the hands of this individual. Fifty years ago, calluses identified a person as a worker. Also, I would like to remind you that after the wars that engulfed the whole world – the civil wars that led to the founding of the World Federation – human life was declared inviolable by the Decree of November 7, 1965. At the same time I must inform you of the objection raised by the Bureau of Epidemiology, which fears the spreading of those bacteria known to have infected the inhabitants of what was then Russia. In full awareness of my responsibility, I say to you, as we put this question to the vote: Comrades, remember, remember, and once again remember:

We
are voting
for a human life!

(The lights dim; a high-pitched bell rings; and the text of the resolution appears on the movie screen; the SPEAKER *reads it aloud.)*

"In the interests of investigating the working habits of the proletariat – in the interests of a graphic comparative study of mores – we demand resurrection!"

(VOICES *from half of the loudspeakers:* "He's right! Adopt the motion!" *Other* VOICES: "Reject it!" *The* VOICES *die out immediately; the screen darkens. A second bell rings, and another resolution is flashed onto the screen. The* SPEAKER *reads it aloud.)*

"Resolution of the public-health stations of the metallurgical and chemical plants of the Don Basin: With a view to avoiding the danger of spreading the bacteria of braggadocio and bootlicking typical of the year 1929, we demand that the exhibit be kept in its frozen state."

(VOICES *from the loudspeakers:* "Reject it!" *Isolated shouts:* "Adopt it!")

SPEAKER

Are there any further resolutions or amendments?

(The screen lights up again, and the SPEAKER *reads from it.)*

"The farming regions of Siberia request that the resurrection be carried out in the fall, when the field work is done, so as to facilitate attendance by the broad masses of interested people."

(An overwhelming majority of the VOICES *from the loudspeakers:* "No! Reject it!" *The bulbs light up.)*

SPEAKER

I put it to a vote. All in favor of the first resolution please raise their hands!

(The great majority of the iron hands are raised.)

All right. Now, all those in favor of the amendment from Siberia!

(Two lone hands are raised.)

The Assembly of the Federation has voted for Re-surrection!

(A roar from all of the loudspeakers: "Hurrah!" *The* VOICES *fade out.)*

The session is closed!

(REPORTERS *surge in through the swinging doors. The* SPEAKER, *unable to restrain himself, shouts in all directions.)*

Resurrection! Resurrection! Resurrection!

(The REPORTERS *take microphones out of their pockets, shouting as they move along.)*

FIRST REPORTER

Hello? 472.5 kilocycles . . . *The Arctic Izvestia* . . . Resurrection!

SECOND REPORTER

Hello? Hello? 376 kilocycles . . . *The Vitebsk Evening Pravda* . . . Resurrection!

THIRD REPORTER

Hello? Hello? Hello! 211 kilocycles . . . *The Warsaw Komsomol Pravda* . . . Resurrection!

FOURTH REPORTER

The Armavir Literary Weekly . . . Hello? Hello?

FIFTH REPORTER

Hello? Hello? Hello! 44 kilocycles . . . *The Chicago Soviet News* . . . Resurrection!

SIXTH REPORTER

Hello? Hello? Hello! 115 kilocycles . . . *The Roman Red Gazette* . . . Resurrection!

SEVENTH REPORTER

Hello? Hello? Hello! 78 kilocycles . . . *The Shanghai Pauper* . . . Resurrection!

EIGHTH REPORTER

Hello? Hello? Hello! 220 kilocycles . . . *The Madrid Milkmaid* . . . Resurrection!

NINTH REPORTER

Hello? Hello? Hello! 11 kilocycles . . . *The Kabul Pioneer* . . . Resurrection!

(NEWSBOYS *hurry in with sheets fresh from the press.)*

FIRST NEWSBOY

To unfreeze
or not to unfreeze?
Editorials in verse
or in prose, as you please.

SECOND NEWSBOY

Worldwide poll
on a critical question:

Is bootlicking still
a contagious infection?

THIRD NEWSBOY

Features on ancient
guitars, "romances,"
And other
methods
of drugging the masses.

FOURTH NEWSBOY

The latest news! Interview! Interview!

FIFTH NEWSBOY

Get the full list
of the foulest words yet!
It's OK to read 'em
in *The Science Gazette.*

SIXTH NEWSBOY

Latest news from the radio!

SEVENTH NEWSBOY

Theoretical discussion
of an ancient question:
Does smoking
give elephants
indigestion?

EIGHTH NEWSBOY

You'll cry
and you'll laugh till you get the colic:
Read what is meant
by the word "alcoholic"!

SCENE VI

A sliding door of frosted glass; through the wall the gleam of metal parts of medical apparatus can be glimpsed. Standing in front of the door are the PROFESSOR *and his elderly female assistant, recognizable as* ZOYA BEREZKINA. *Both wear white hospital smocks.*

ZOYA

Comrade! Comrade Professor! Please don't go ahead with this experiment! If you do, that bad business will start all over again!

PROFESSOR

Comrade Berezkina, you've taken to in the past. You're talking a language I can't understand – just like a dictionary of obsolete words. What does "bad business" mean? *(Looks through a dictionary.)* Business . . . business . . . Let's see. Bohemia . . . bubliki . . . Bulgakov . . . bureaucracy . . . business. Ah, yes! "Business, comma, bad: a kind of human activity that obstructed all other activity."

ZOYA

Fifty years ago, that "activity" almost cost me my life. I even went so far as . . . well, I tried to commit suicide.

PROFESSOR

Suicide? What's suicide? *(Looks in the dictionary.)* Suffragette . . . sugar . . . suggestive. . . . Here it is – "suicide." *(In amazement)* You shot yourself? On orders from a court? From a revolutionary tribunal?

ZOYA

No. On my own.

PROFESSOR

On your own? Out of carelessness?

ZOYA

No. Out of love.

PROFESSOR

Oh, come now! Out of love, one bears children, or builds a bridge. . . . But you. . . . Well, I must say!

ZOYA

Please let me out of this. I can't go through with it!

PROFESSOR

It certainly is – how did you put it? – "a bad business." I must say! "A bad business!" Society expects you to manifest all the feelings you can muster so as to make it as easy as possible for this patient we are about to defrost to overcome fifty anabiotic years. Oh, my, yes! Your presence is very, very important! I'm so glad that he and she turned up and came here! He is he, and you are she! Tell me, were his eyelids fragile? They might break in the course of rapid unfreezing.

ZOYA

Comrade Professor, how can I remember eyelids that existed fifty years ago?

PROFESSOR

What? Fifty years ago? That was only yesterday! How do you think I remember the color of the hairs on the tail of a mastodon that lived a half-million years ago? I must say! And do you remember whether his nostrils were strongly dilated by his breathing in the presence of excited company?

ZOYA

Comrade Professor, how could I possibly remember? It's been thirty years since people dilated their nostrils in such situations.

PROFESSOR

All right, all right! And do you know the size of his stomach and liver – in the event of the excretion of a possible content of alcohol that might ignite at the high voltage we must use?

ZOYA

How can I remember such things, Comrade Professor? I recall that he had a stomach of sorts –

PROFESSOR

Oh, you don't remember anything, Comrade Berezkina! But at least you can tell me whether he was impulsive, can't you?

ZOYA

I don't know. Maybe he was . . . but not with me.

PROFESSOR

I see! I see! I'm afraid that while we're defrosting him, you've been freezing up. Oh, my, yes! . . . Well, let's get on with it.

(Pushes a button, and the glass door slides back quietly. Stage center, on an operating table, is a shining, zinc-covered, coffin-like box. Along its sides are faucets with pails under them; electric wires lead into it. Oxygen tanks here and there. Six DOCTORS, *white-clad and calm, stand around the box. Upstage, in front of the box, are six washstands. Six towels hang from an invisible wire, as though in midair.)*

PROFESSOR *(going from doctor to doctor; to the first)*

Switch on the current when I give the signal. *(To the second)* Bring the temperature up to ninety-seven degrees at the rate of one-tenth of a degree per second. *(To the third)* Is the oxygen tank ready? *(To the fourth)* Let the water drain off gradually as you replace the ice with air-pressure. *(To the fifth)* Raise the lid immediately! *(To the sixth)* Watch the stages of his revival in the mirror.

(The DOCTORS *nod their heads in acknowledgment and take their places.)*

Let's go!

(The current is switched on, and they watch the temperature. The SIXTH DOCTOR *keeps his eyes glued to a mirror in the right end of the box.)*

SIXTH DOCTOR

His natural color is coming back!

(A pause)

He's free from ice!

(A pause)

His chest is heaving! *(Alarmed)* Professor, just look at those abnormal spasms!

PROFESSOR *(approaches and takes a close look; in a calm voice)*

The movements are normal – he's scratching himself.

Obviously, the parasites typically found on such individuals are reviving.

SIXTH DOCTOR

Professor, something strange is happening! His left hand is moving away from his body.

PROFESSOR *(taking a close look)*

He was a music lover – what they used to call a "sensitive soul." In ancient times there was a man named Stradivarius and a man named Utkin. Stradivarius made violins, and Utkin made those other things – they called them guitars.[1]

(The PROFESSOR *checks the thermometer and the apparatus showing the blood pressure.)*

FIRST DOCTOR

Ninety-seven degrees.

SECOND DOCTOR

Pulse sixty-eight.

SIXTH DOCTOR

Respiration even.

PROFESSOR

To your places!

(The DOCTORS *walk away from the box. The lid opens immediately, and* PRISYPKIN *sits up, disheveled and amazed. Still clutching his guitar, he looks around.)*

PRISYPKIN

I sure had a good sleep! My apologies, comrades, but I was pretty drunk, you know. . . . What police station is this, anyway? Am I in the cooler?

PROFESSOR

This isn't a cooler, it's a defroster. We melted the ice off your cutaneous integument, which you had allowed to get frostbitten.

PRISYPKIN

What? *You're* the ones who are frostbitten! We'll soon see who was really drunk! You doctors are always sniffing around the alcohol. Anyway, I can always prove my identity. I've got my papers on me. *(Climbs out of the box and turns his pockets inside out.)* Seventeen rubles and sixty kopecks. *Going through the contents of his pockets.*

The Revolutionary Fighters' Fund? Paid. The National Defense Fund? Check. The Anti-illiteracy Campaign? OK. . . . What's this? A marriage certificate! *(Whistles)* That's right – I got married yesterday! "Where are you now? Who is kissing your fingertips?" Oh, there'll be hell to pay when I get home! . . . Here's the receipt from the attendants, and here's my union card. *(He happens to notice the calendar; rubs his eyes, and looks around him, horror-struck.) May 12, 1979!* I'm fifty years behind on my union dues! All those forms to fill out – those explanations! My District Office! My Central Committee! My God! My wife! Let me out of here! *(Shakes hands with the doctors and heads for the door.)*

> *(*ZOYA, *very upset, follows him; the six* DOCTORS *crowd around the PROFESSOR and speak in chorus.)*

DOCTORS

What was that he was doing with our hands? Grabbing and shaking them, shaking and grabbing. . . .

PROFESSOR

It's an unhygienic custom they had in ancient times.

PRISYPKIN *(bumping into* ZOYA*)*

And just who might you be, Madame Citizen? Who am I? Where am I? You aren't by any chance the mother of Zoya Berezkina? *(Hears the screeching of a siren, and turns his head.)* Where *am* I, anyway? Where did they put me? What place is this? Moscow? Paris? New York? . . . Hey, cabby!

> *(The honking of automobile horns can be heard.)*

No people, no horses! Just cars, cars, and more cars! *(Backs up against the door; scratches his back on it; feels around with his five fingers; turns around, and sees a bedbug crawling from his collar onto the white wall.)* Oh, bedbug! Beddie-buggie! Little bastard! *(Strums on his guitar and sings)*

Don't go away –
Stay here with me awhile. . . .

> *(Tries to catch the bedbug in his fingers; it gets away.)*

We have parted, like ships on the sea.

He got away! I'm all alone!
But no one answers me,
and again I am alone. . . .
Alone!

Cabby! Automobiles! . . . Seventeen Lunacharsky Street – without my bags! *(Puts his hand to his head and faints, falling into the arms of* ZOYA, *who has run out the door after him.)*

SCENE VII

Stage center, a triangular plaza, with three artificial trees. The first tree has square green leaves; on the leaves are huge plates containing tangerines. On the second tree are paper plates with apples. The third tree is green, with pine cones which are actually open bottles of perfume. To the right and left, glass walls of buildings. Long benches run along the sides of the plaza. Enter a REPORTER, *followed by four* MEN *and* WOMEN.

REPORTER

Let's go over here, comrades, in the shade. I'll tell you about all these amazing, ominous events in order of their occurrence. In the first place. . . . Pass me some tangerines, will you? The municipal authorities were right to make the trees tangerine today. Yesterday all we had was pears —no juice, no taste, and no food value.

(*A* GIRL *takes a plate of tangerines from the tree. The people on the bench peel and eat them, looking expectantly at the* REPORTER.)

FIRST MAN

Well, come on, comrade! Tell us the whole story in detail and in chronological order.

REPORTER

Well, you see. . . . How juicy each little section is! Don't you want some? . . . Well, all right, I'll tell you. But how impatient you are! Naturally, as dean of the press corps, I know the whole story. . . . Say, look at that! Just look!

(*A man with a full case of thermometers walks past rapidly.*)

He's a veterinarian. The epidemic is spreading. When it was left alone, that resurrected mammal made friends with all the domestic animals in the skyscraper, and now all the dogs have gone mad. It taught them to stand up on their hind legs. Now the dogs don't bark or frisk about any more. All they do is hold down their jobs. They pester everybody at the dinner table, fawning and licking boots. The doctors say that any human beings bitten by these dogs will show all the first symptoms of epidemic bootlicking.

MEN AND WOMEN

O-o-oh!

REPORTER

Look! Look over there!

(A MAN *staggers past, loaded with hampers full of bottled beer.)*

STAGGERING MAN *(singing)*

Back in the nineteenth century,
A man could live most royally,
Drinking vodka, beer, and rum
Till his nose looked like a nice, ripe plum.

REPORTER

Just look at the man! He's sick – done! He was one of the hundred and seventy-five workers at the Second Medical Laboratory. To make things easier for the resurrected mammal during its transitional stage of existence, the doctors prescribed a beverage that is poisonous in large doses and revolting in small ones; beer, it's called. The noxious fumes made the doctors dizzy, and some of them mistakenly took a swig of that refreshing mixture. Since then there have been three complete turnovers of the laboratory personnel, and five hundred twenty workers have been hospitalized. But the terrible wave of the epidemic is still foaming, seething, and mowing people down.

MEN AND WOMEN

O-o-o-oh!

MAN *(dreamily and yearningly)*

I'm ready to sacrifice myself for science! They can inoculate me with that mysterious disease if they want to.

REPORTER

So you're ready! Another ready victim! . . . Quiet, everybody! Don't startle that sleepwalker coming our way!

(A GIRL *stumbles by, trying to do the foxtrot and the Charleston at the same time, while mumbling verses from a slim volume of poetry held between two fingers of her outstretched hand. Between two fingers of her other hand she holds an imaginary rose, which she brings up to her nose and sniffs.)*

The poor thing! She lives next door to that demented mammal. At night, while the city slept, she would hear through the wall the twanging of his guitar, followed by long, heart-rending sighs and a kind of singsong sobbing. What was it they used to call such things – "love laments," wasn't it? The more she heard, the worse things got, and the poor girl began to lose her mind. Her parents were terribly upset. They called in some medical experts for a consultation. The professors said it was an acute attack of "love" – the name given to a disease of ancient times when sexual energy, which should be rationally distributed over one's entire lifetime, is suddenly concentrated into one inflammation lasting a week, leading to absurd and incredible behavior.

GIRL *([on the bench] covering her face with her hands)*

I'd better not look any more! I can just feel those terrible "love" microbes spreading through the air!

REPORTER

She's ready, too – another ready victim! This epidemic is growing to the size of an ocean!

(Thirty CHORUS GIRLS *dance onto the stage.)*

Look at that thirty-headed sixty-legged creature! Just imagine! That raising of the legs *(Turns to the audience)* used to be called art!

(A COUPLE *enters, doing the foxtrot.)*

The epidemic has reached its – its – what has it reached, anyway? *(Looks in a dictionary.)* Its a-po-gee. That thing there is a bisexual quadruped.

(The ZOO DIRECTOR *comes rushing in, carrying a*

small glass case. After him comes a crowd with telescopes, cameras, and fire ladders.)

DIRECTOR *(to everybody)*

Did you see it? Did you see it? Where is it? Oh, so you didn't see anything! A party of hunters said they saw it here about fifteen minutes ago. They said it was climbing up toward the fourth floor. Assuming its average speed to be about one and a half meters per hour, it can't have gone very far. Comrades, search the walls immediately!

(The people in the crowd pull their telescopes out to full length. Those on the bench jump to their feet and strain to see, shading their eyes.)

VOICES

You think that's the way to find it?
The thing to do is put a naked person on a mattress in every window. Because humans are what it goes for.
Don't shout, you'll scare it away!
If *I* find it, I won't give it to *anybody!*
You wouldn't dare! It's communal property!

EXCITED VOICE

I found it! Here it is! It's crawling!

(All the telescopes and binoculars are focused on one point. There is a silence, disturbed only by the clicking and whirring of cameras, both motion picture and regular.)

PROFESSOR *(in a strangled whisper)*

Yes, that's it! Set up an ambush and post the guards! Firemen, over here!

(People with nets surround the spot. The FIREMEN *put up their ladder, and people climb up in Indian file.)*

DIRECTOR *(lowering his telescope, in a plaintive tone)*

It got away! . . . Got over to the next wall. . . . SOS! . . . It'll fall and get killed! Heroes! Volunteers! Daredevils! . . . This way!

(The ladder is put up against the other wall, and people clamber up. Others watch, petrified.)

EXCITED VOICE FROM ABOVE

I got it! Hurrah!

DIRECTOR

Quick! But be careful! Don't let it get away! And don't break its legs!

(The insect is passed down the ladder from hand to hand, finally reaching the hands of the DIRECTOR. *He puts it in the glass case, and raises the case over his head.)*

Many thanks, all you humble servitors of science! Our zoo is the recipient of both happiness and a masterpiece! . . . We have captured a very rare specimen of an extinct insect which was extremely popular in the early days of the century. Our city may be justly proud of itself. Scientists and tourists will come here in throngs. . . . Right here in my hands I hold the only extant specimen of the *Bedbugus normalis.* . . . Stand back, citizens! The insect has gone to sleep. The insect has crossed its legs. The insect wants to rest. I hereby invite all of you to the formal opening of an exhibit in the Zoological Garden. The act of capture – so very important, and the cause of such great anxiety – has been completed!

SCENE VIII

A room with smooth, opalescent, translucent walls. Along the top of the walls, a band of pale-blue light from an overhead source. On the left, a large window, with a drafting board in front of it. A radio, a motion-picture screen, three or four books. On the right, a bed unfolded from the wall. On the bed, lying under a very clean blanket, is a very dirty PRISYPKIN. *Electric fans.* PRISYPKIN*'s corner of the room is a mess. The table is strewn with cigarette butts and bottles lying on their sides; a scrap of pink paper has been pasted on the bulb of the reading lamp.* PRISYPKIN *is groaning. A* DOCTOR *is pacing the room nervously.*

PROFESSOR *(entering)*

How are things going with the patient?

DOCTOR

I don't know about the patient, but with me things are disgusting! If you don't arrange for a new shift in here every half hour, he'll infect all of us. Every time he breathes, it makes me weak in the knees. I've already installed seven fans to clear the air of his exhalations.

PRISYPKIN

Oo-oo-ooh!

(The PROFESSOR *rushes over to him.)*

Professor! Oh, pro-fess-ssor!

(The PROFESSOR *takes one good sniff and staggers back in a faint, clawing at the air.)*

I need a shot – the hair of the dog!

(The PROFESSOR *pours some beer into a glass – just enough to cover the bottom – and gives it to him.* PRISYPKIN *pulls himself up on his elbows. Reproachfully.)*

You resurrected me, and now you're insulting me! Why, that's like lemonade for an elephant.

PROFESSOR

Society hopes to bring you up to the human level.

PRISYPKIN

To hell with society, and to hell with you, too! I never asked you to resurrect me. Freeze me back where I was!

PROFESSOR

I don't understand what you're talking about. Our lives belong to the collective, and neither I nor anyone else has the right to –

PRISYPKIN

But what kind of a life is it when you can't even pin up a picture of your girl friend on the wall? The thumbtacks break on this damned glass wall here. . . . Comrade Professor, give me some more hair of the dog.

PROFESSOR *(fills the glass)*

All right, just so you don't breathe in my direction.

*(*ZOYA *enters with two bundles of books. The* DOCTORS *talk with her in a whisper, and then go out.)*

ZOYA *(sits down next to* PRISYPKIN'S *bed and unties the books)*

I don't know if these will suit you. They didn't have what you asked for, and nobody knows anything about it. Only the manuals on horticulture say anything about roses. And fantasies are mentioned only in the medical books – in the section on dreaming. But now here are two very interesting books from about the same period. The first one is translated from the English. It's by Herbert Hoover, and it's called *An Ex-President Speaks.*

PRISYPKIN *(takes the book, then throws it to one side)*

No, that one's not for the heart. I want something that makes my heart stand still.

ZOYA

Here's the other one. It's by somebody named Mussolini. The title is *Letters from Exile.*

PRISYPKIN *(takes it, then throws it to one side)*

No, that's not for the soul. Don't bother me with your crude propaganda books! I want something that plucks at the strings of my –

ZOYA

I don't know what you're talking about. "Makes my heart stand still"; "Plucks at the strings. . . ." What is all that?

PRISYPKIN

What *is* all that? What did we fight for? Why did we spill our blood if I, a leader in our new society, can't enjoy myself doing the new dance steps, and so on?

ZOYA

I demonstrated your bodily movements for the director of the Central Institute of Calisthenics. He says he used to see things like that in the old collections of French postcards, but that today there isn't even anybody left we could ask about things like that. There *are* a couple of old women who remember those dances, but they can't demonstrate them on account of their rheumatism.

PRISYPKIN

Then what good was it for me to acquire such a thoroughly elegant education? *Working* was a thing I could do even before the Revolution.

ZOYA

Tomorrow I'll take you to see a dance performed. Ten thousand male and female workers will move across the public square. It will be a joyous rehearsal of a new system for field work on the farms.

PRISYPKIN

Comrades, I object! I didn't unfreeze just so you could dry me up! *(Throws off the blanket, leaps out of bed, grabs a bundle of books, and shakes them out of the paper in which they are wrapped. He is about to tear up the paper – a large handbill – but suddenly looks more closely at the printing on it, then goes from one lamp* [*to another to read it better.*]) Where did you get this?

ZOYA

They were handing them out to everybody in the streets. The people at the library must have put some in the books.

PRISYPKIN

Saved! Hurrah! *(He rushes out the door, waving the handbill like a flag.)*

ZOYA *(alone)*

Just think! Instead of living and moving ahead for fifty years, I might have died fifty years back on account of that rat!

SCENE IX

A zoo. In the center, on a platform, a cage under a cloth cover, draped with flags. Behind the cage, two trees; and behind them, cages with elephants and giraffes. To the left of the cage, a speakers' platform; to the right, a reviewing stand for dignitaries. MUSICIANS *are standing around the cage, and* SPECTATORS *are approaching it in little groups. The* MASTER OF CEREMONIES *and his* ATTENDANTS, *wearing armbands, are assigning people to their places in accordance with their ages and occupations.*

MASTER OF CEREMONIES

This way, comrades of the foreign press! Closer to the rostrum! Move to one side and leave room for the Brazilians! Their airship is just now landing at the Central Airport. *(Steps back and admires his work.)* Negro Comrades, mix in with the British so as to form attractively colored groups. Their Anglo-Saxon pallor will make your complexions show to even better advantage. . . . You students move over to the left. Three old ladies and three old men from the Centenarians Union have been assigned to you. They will supplement the professors' explanations with eyewitness accounts.

(The OLD LADIES *and* OLD MEN *are brought in in wheelchairs.)*

FIRST OLD LADY

I remember like it was now –

FIRST OLD MAN

No, I'm the one that remembers like it was now!

SECOND OLD LADY

You remember like it was now, but *I* remember how it was before.

SECOND OLD MAN

But I remember, like it was now, how it was before.

THIRD OLD LADY

And I remember how it was even before that – long, long before that!

THIRD OLD MAN

Well, *I* remember like it was now *and* how it was before.

MASTER OF CEREMONIES

Quiet there, eyewitnesses! No lisping, please! Gangway, comrades! Make way for the children! Over here, comrades. Step along, there! Step along!

CHILDREN *(marching in a column and singing)*

We pass
all our tests;
We get "A"s on our papers.
But the thing
we like best
Is to go
for a caper.
We're through with our reading
and writing and math:
Now it's time to be feeding
the bears and giraffes!
We'll see
all our furry
And furless
friends, too!
Come along!
Let's all hurry –
Let's go
to the zoo!

MASTER OF CEREMONIES

Regulated doses of exotic products, together with scientific instruments, may be obtained from zoo employees – and from no one else – by citizens desirous of giving pleasure to the animals on exhibit, or of utilizing such products for scientific purposes. Amateurism or excess in the use of these doses may be fatal. Therefore, please use only the products and equipment supplied by the Central Medical Institute and the Municipal Laboratory of Precision Engineering.

(ATTENDANTS *walk about in the zoo and the theater.)*

FIRST ATTENDANT

Can you see germs
with spectacles?
Don't be an ass!
Get a microscope
or
a magnifying glass!

SECOND ATTENDANT

In case you get spit on,
be sure
to use phenol.
It comes recommended
by good Dr. Venal.

THIRD ATTENDANT

Feeding time at the zoo
is a memorable scene
If you give the beasts
liquor
and nicotine!

FOURTH ATTENDANT

Give the animals vodka –
a sure guarantee
Of the gout, enlarged liver,
and idiocy!

FIFTH ATTENDANT

Give the beasts cigarettes,
and as sure as your nose is
On your face,
they'll come down
with
arteriosclerosis!

SIXTH ATTENDANT

Guard your ears
against language
that shouldn't be heard!
These earphones
screen out
every coarse, filthy word!

MASTER OF CEREMONIES *(clearing a way to the speakers' platform)*

The Comrade Chairman of the City Council and his closest colleagues have taken time off from their very important work to attend our ceremony. Here they come now, in step to the strains of our ancient national anthem. Let's welcome our dear comrades!

(Everyone applauds, as a group of OFFICIALS *cross the stage, bowing with dignity and singing.)*

OFFICIALS

The burden of our duties
Hasn't turned us gray.
There's a time for doing,
And a time for play.
Greetings from the Council,
Bold huntsmen of the zoo!
We're the fathers of the city,
And we're mighty proud of you!

CHAIRMAN OF THE CITY COUNCIL *(mounts the speakers' platform and waves a flag; everyone quiets down)*

Comrades, I declare the ceremony open! The times we live in are fraught with deep turmoil and experiences of an inner nature. External events are rare. Mankind, exhausted by the events of preceding ages, is grateful for this relative peace. Still, we never refuse to watch a spectacle which, however extravagant it may seem outwardly, contains a deep scientific truth hidden beneath its iridescent plumage. The melancholy events we have witnessed in our city were the result of negligence in admitting two parasites within its precincts. Through my efforts, and through the efforts of world medicine, these crises have been surmounted. However, these incidents, as faint reminders of the past, emphasize the horror of those days and the intensity and hardships of the cultural struggle fought by the workers of the world.

May the hearts and souls of our youth be strengthened by these evil examples!

I want now to express my gratitude to the next speaker, our famous director here at the zoo, who untangled the meaning of these strange events and turned a baleful phenomenon into a gay and instructive entertainment. All hail!

(Everyone cheers; the band strikes up a fanfare as the DIRECTOR *mounts the speakers' platform, bowing.)*

DIRECTOR

Comrades! I am both delighted and embarrassed by your kindness. Without minimizing my own part in the matter, I would nevertheless like to thank the dedicated workers of the Hunters' Union, who are the real heroes of the capture. Also, I would like to thank the esteemed professor from the Institute of Human Resurrection, who vanquished the chill of death. I must point out, however, that the esteemed professor's first mistake was the indirect cause of our misfortunes. On the basis of certain mimetic characteristics of the defrosted mammal – its calluses, clothing, and so on – the esteemed professor mistakenly assigned it to the species *Homo sapiens,* and even to its highest division, the working class. As for my own success, I do not attribute it entirely to my long experience with animals, and my understanding of their psychology. Chance came to my aid. A vague, subconscious hope kept whispering to me: "Write up an announcement, and publish it!" So I did. Here it is:

"In accordance with principles of the zoo, I am seeking a live human body to be constantly bitten by a newly acquired insect in order to assure the sustenance and growth of that insect under the normal conditions to which it is accustomed."

VOICE FROM THE CROWD

Oh! How terrible!

DIRECTOR

I am well aware that it's terrible. In fact, I had no real faith in my own absurd idea . . . until suddenly, the creature appeared! It looked almost human – you know, like you or me –

CHAIRMAN OF THE CITY COUNCIL *(ringing his bell)*

Comrade Director, I must call you to order!

DIRECTOR

Oh, I'm sorry! I apologize. And so, of course, I immediately concluded, on the basis of interrogation and comparative bestiology, that the creature was a frightful anthropoid simulator, and that they are the most paralyzing of parasites. I shall avoid going into details, since you will soon see them for yourselves in this most amazing cage.

There are two parasites, differing in size but the same in essence: the famous *Bedbugus normalis* and – and the *Philistinius vulgaris*. Both have their habitat in the moldy mattresses of time. *Bedbugus normalis*, when it has guzzled and gorged on the body of a single human being, falls under the bed. *Philistinius vulgaris*, when it has guzzled and gorged on the body of all mankind, falls on top of the bed. That's the only difference!

When the toiling humanity of the Revolution was writhing and scratching itself, scraping away the filth, these parasites built their nests and homes in that same filth, beat their wives, swore by false gods,[1] and took their blissful ease in the shady tents of their own riding breeches.[2] But of the two types, *Philistinius vulgaris* is the more frightful. He lured his victims with monstrous mimetic powers, sometimes in the guise of a chirruping rhymester, sometimes as crooning songbird. In those days even their clothes were mimetic: in their wing ties, swallow-tailed coats, and starched white breasts, they looked just like birds. These birds built nests in box seats at the theaters; perched on oaks at the opera; rubbed their legs together in the ballet, to the strains of the "Internationale"; hung head down from the twigs of their verses; made Tolstoy look like Marx; complained and shrieked in disgustingly large flocks; and – please forgive the expression, but this lecture is scientific – excreted in quantities which could not be considered mere small bird droppings.

Comrades! . . . But no matter: you'll see for yourselves.

(Gives a signal, and the cage is unveiled by ATTENDANTS. *On a pedestal, the glass case with the bedbug; behind it, a dais on which is a double bed. On the bed,* PRISYPKIN *with his guitar. In the top of the cage, a lamp with a yellow shade. Above* PRISYPKIN'*s head, a radiant halo consisting of postcards arranged fanwise. On the floor, bottles – some upright, some on their sides. Spittoons are placed all around the cage. On the sides, filters, air-conditioners, and signs. The signs read:* (1) "BEWARE – IT SPITS!"; (2) "IF YOU HAVEN'T BEEN ANNOUNCED, DON'T COME IN!"; (3) "PROTECT YOUR EARS – IT CURSES!" *The band plays a fanfare. Bengal lights. The crowd draws back, then comes up to the cage again, struck dumb with delight.)*

PRISYPKIN

I recall an ancient house
That stood on Lunacharsky Street:
The stairs were broad and marvelous,
The windows elegant and neat.

DIRECTOR

Come closer, comrades. Don't be frightened – it's completely tame. Closer, closer! No need to worry. There are four filters inside the cage to filter out the bad language, and the few words that do get through are perfectly proper. The filters are cleaned every day by special attendants in gas masks. . . . Look! Now it's going to "smoke," as they used to say.

VOICE FROM THE CROWD

Oh, how terrible.

DIRECTOR

There's nothing to be afraid of. Now it's going to "have a snort," as they used to say. Skripkin, take a swig!

(SKRIPKIN *reaches for a bottle of vodka.)*

VOICE FROM THE CROWD

Oh, don't do that! Don't torture the poor beast!

DIRECTOR

Comrades, there's nothing to be frightened of – it's tame. Just watch now, and I'll lead it out onto the platform. *(Goes to the cage, puts on gloves, checks his gun, and opens the door. He leads* SKRIPKIN *out to the speakers' platform and turns him around to face the dignitaries on the reviewing stand.)* All right. Now say a few words, imitating the human expression, voice, and language.

SKRIPKIN *(stands obediently, clears his throat, raises his guitar, then suddenly turns and looks at the audience. His expression changes, and becomes joyful. He pushes the* DIRECTOR *to one side, throws down his guitar, and shouts to the audience)*

Citizens! My people! My own people! Dear ones! How did you get here? So many of you! When did they unfreeze you? Why am I alone in the cage? Dear ones, my people! Come in with me! Why am I suffering? Citizens! –

VOICES OF GUESTS

The children! Get them out of here!

Muzzle it! Put a muzzle on it!

Oh, how horrible!

Professor, stop these proceedings!

But please don't shoot it! Please!

(The DIRECTOR *comes running back to the platform, carrying a fan and accompanied by two* ATTENDANTS. *The* ATTENDANTS *drag* SKRIPKIN *off. The* DIRECTOR *ventilates the platform. The band strikes up a fanfare. The* ATTENDANTS *cover the cage.)*

DIRECTOR

I beg your pardon, Comrades. I apologize. . . . The insect was tired. The noise and bright lights brought on hallucinations. Please be calm. It was just a fantasy. The creature will calm down tomorrow. . . . Leave quietly, citizens. See you tomorrow! Band leader, play a march!

CURTAIN

1928–1929

THE BATHHOUSE

A Drama in Six Acts, with a Circus and Fireworks

Characters[1]

Comrade POBEDONOSIKOV, Chief, Federal Bureau of Coordination; abbreviated title: Fedburoco

POLYA, his wife

Comrade OPTIMISTENKO, his administrative secretary

ISAAC BELVEDONSKY, a painter of portraits and battle scenes; a practitioner of photographic realism

Comrade MOMENTALNIKOV, a reporter

Mr. PONT KICH, a foreigner

A TYPIST, Comrade UNDERTON

NOCHKIN, an embezzler

Comrade VELOSIPEDKIN, a trouble-shooter from the Young Communist League

Comrade CHUDAKOV, an inventor

Madame MEZALYANSOVA, an interpreter from VOKS[2]

Comrade FOSKIN
Comrade DVOYKIN } workmen
Comrade TROYKIN

PETITIONERS

CHAIRMAN OF THE TENANTS' COMMITTEE [in an apartment house]

DIRECTOR OF THE PLAY

IVAN IVANOVICH

A QUEUE OF PEOPLE

A POLICEMAN

AN USHER

THE PHOSPHORESCENT WOMAN

ACT I

CHUDAKOV's workshop in the basement of an apartment building. On the right and left, work tables. Blueprints hang down from the walls and ceiling, and are strewn all over the place. In the center, Comrade FOSKIN is soldering an invisible object with a blowtorch. CHUDAKOV goes from one light bulb to another, checking the blueprints.

VELOSIPEDKIN *(rushing in)*

What's new? Does the vile Volga still empty into the Caspian Sea?

CHUDAKOV *(waving a blueprint)*

Yes, but it won't for long. Better pawn your watch or sell it.

VELOSIPEDKIN

I'm in luck – I haven't even bought one yet.

CHUDAKOV

Well, don't! Don't buy a watch under any circumstances! Before long those flat, tick-tocking things will be more ridiculous than wood torches at the Dnieper Power Plant – more useless than an ox team on a highway.[1]

VELOSIPEDKIN

Why? Has Switzerland been cut down to the size of an insect?

CHUDAKOV

Stop clicking your tongue like an abacus counting up the petty political gains of the present day! My idea is much grander. Henceforth the Volga River of Time, into which, by our birth, we were cast like so many logs for floating – cast, I say, to flounder and float downstream – that river will be subject to our control! I shall compel time to stop – or else to rush off in any desired direction and at any desired speed. People will be able to climb out of days like passengers out of a streetcar or bus. With my machine you can bring one second of happiness to a halt and enjoy it for a whole month – or until it bores you. With my machine you can make long-drawn-out years of sorrow flash by like a whirlwind. You just duck down, and the projectile of the sun will whiz over your head a hundred times a minute without once wounding or even grazing you, thus bringing your days of gloom to an end. Just look! The fireworks fantasies of H. G. Wells, the futuristic brain of Einstein, and the bestial hibernating habits of bears and yogis – all these are compressed, squeezed together, and combined in my machine!

VELOSIPEDKIN

Almost everything you say is beyond me, and I certainly don't *see* anything at all.

CHUDAKOV

Then put on your goggles! You're blinded by all those crystal and platinum bands – by the brilliance of those crisscrossed rays of light. Do you see anything now? *Do* you?

VELOSIPEDKIN

Well, yes, I do.

CHUDAKOV

Look closely. Do you see those two little bars, one vertical and one horizontal, with graduations like a ruler or a scale?

VELOSIPEDKIN

Yes, I see them.

CHUDAKOV

With those little rulers you measure off the cube of the requisite space. Now look again. Do you see that dial there?

VELOSIPEDKIN

Yes, I see it.

CHUDAKOV

Well, with that control switch you isolate the occluded space, and you cut off all currents of the earth's gravitation from all other gravitational forces. Then, with those funny-looking levers there, you put in the speed and direction of time.

VELOSIPEDKIN

I get it! Wonderful! Terrific! This means that . . . well, let's suppose there's an All-Union Congress on the Problem of How to Hush Up All Problems Raised. And, furthermore, that the welcoming speech on behalf of the National Academy of Scientific Arts is to be given, naturally, by National Comrade Kogan.[2] As soon as he begins with: "Comrades, through the tentacles of world imperialism there runs, like a red thread, a wave of . . ." I'll switch him off from the presidium and cut in time at a speed of a hundred and fifty minutes per quarter-hour. He'll go on sweating and welcoming, welcoming and sweating, for an hour and a half. But with the audience it'll be different. One minute they'll see the academician just opening his mouth, and the next they'll hear deafening applause. Then they'll all heave a sigh of relief, hoist their fresh, unwearied behinds up from their seats, and get back to work – right?

CHUDAKOV

Ugh, how loathsome! Do you *have* to tell me about this person named Kogan? I'm giving you an explanation of universal relativity – how the definition of time is converted from a metaphysical substance, a noumenon, into a reality subject to chemical and physical action.

VELOSIPEDKIN

And what do I say? Here's what I say! You go ahead and build a real station, with full chemical and physical action, and we'll wire it up to – let's say – all the baby-chick incubators. In fifteen minutes we'll raise an eighteen-pound chicken. We'll put an electric plug under her wing, and switch off time. Then: sit right there, chickie, and wait until you're fried and eaten!

CHUDAKOV

What incubators? What chickens? I'm telling you –

VELOSIPEDKIN

OK, OK! You can think in terms of elephants or giraffes if you want to – if little barnyard beasts aren't good enough for you. But the rest of us will go ahead and use all these ideas on our little gray baby chicks.

CHUDAKOV

What a petty, vulgar way to look at things! Your practical materialism gives me the feeling you'll soon turn *me* into a chicken! The moment I flap my wings and try to fly, you pluck out my feathers.

VELOSIPEDKIN

All right, all right! Don't get riled up now! If I've plucked out one of your feathers, I apologize. And don't worry: I'll put it back again. Take off! Fly high! Let your fantasies run wild! We're here to encourage your enthusiasm, not to dampen it. So don't be mad at me, old fellow. Go ahead and start your machine – crank it up! What can I do to help?

CHUDAKOV

Watch! I just touch this dial, and time picks up tremendous speed and starts to compress and alter the space we have compartmented here in this insulated chamber. At this very moment I am creating mass unemployment for all prophets, seers, and fortunetellers.

VELOSIPEDKIN

Wait a minute! Let's see what happens if I move over this way. In five minutes I'll probably develop from a member of the Young Communist League into one of those long-bearded Karl Marx types. No, on second thought I'll probably become an old Bolshevik with three hundred years of seniority. Then I can get all your projects approved right away.

CHUDAKOV *(frightened, pulling him away)*

Careful, you madman! In the future they may build a subway through here. If that happens, and you've interposed your puny body in the space where the steel tracks go, you'll be instantly transformed into tooth powder. Besides, the cars of the future subway train may go off the tracks, causing a huge, unprecedented timequake that will smash this whole basement to kingdom come. So right now it's dangerous to go in that direction. What we have to do is wait for the people coming from there. I'll just turn this dial here very slowly, only five years per minute—

FOSKIN

Stop, comrade! Hold it a minute! You're going to

start your machine anyway, so do me a favor and put this government bond in it for me. I'd hate to think I'd bought it and hung on to it this long for nothing. That way, maybe in five minutes it'd be worth a hundred thousand rubles.

VELOSIPEDKIN

Some idea, all right! If we put the bond in, we'll have to put the whole Commissariat of Finance in, too. Otherwise, even if you do make a killing on it, they'll think you're lying and they'll demand documentary proof.

CHUDAKOV

Well, I must say! Here I am breaking open a door into the future, and what do you people do? You bring the whole thing down to the grubby level of money. Phooey on you historical materialists!

FOSKIN

Don't be silly! The only reason I'm in a hurry to make some money on my bond is so you can use it. Do you have enough money for your experiment?

CHUDAKOV

Oh, *money?* Do we have any, I wonder?

VELOSIPEDKIN

Money?

(A knock on the door; enter IVAN IVANOVICH, PONT KICH, MEZALYANSOVA, *and* MOMENTALNIKOV.*)*

MEZALYANSOVA *(to* CHUDAKOV*)*

Vy govoríte po-anglíyski?[3] No? Well, then, *sprechen Sie Deutsch?* Or *parlez-vous français?* No? Just as I suspected! It's all so tiresome! Now I'll have to interpret from our kind of language into that worker-peasant tongue. This is Monsieur Ivan Ivanovich – Comrade Ivan Ivanovich. You of course know Ivan Ivanovich?

IVAN IVANOVICH

How do you do, dear comrade, how do you do? Please don't stand on ceremony! I'm just showing off our achievements – to use a favorite phrase of my friend Max Gorky. I myself sometimes. . . . But then, you know, the work load is so great! We workers and peasants have a need – a crying need – for our own Edison, a Red Edison.

Naturally, what with our growing pains, and the slight defects in the mechanism. . . . Well, you have to break eggs to make an omelet. . . . Just one more effort, boys, and we'll overcome all that! Do you happen to have a telephone here? Oh, no telephone? Well, don't worry, I'll tell my friend Nikolay Ivanovich. He won't turn you down. But if he does, I can go straight to Vladimir Panfilych himself. He'll take care of it, I can assure you. Why, even Semyon Semyonovich is always telling me: "We workers and peasants," he says, "we need our own Edison – a Soviet Edison." Comrade Momentalnikov, we must launch a broad campaign!

MOMENTALNIKOV

Excellency, give your orders!
Our appetite is small.
Just g-g-give us a quota,
And we'll get right on the ball.

MEZALYANSOVA

Meet Monsieur Momentalnikov – Comrade Momentalnikov! A collaborator, a fellow traveler. He saw the Soviet regime was coming, so he joined up. He saw we were coming, so he turned our way. If he sees *they* are coming, he'll leave us.

MOMENTALNIKOV

Absolutely! Absolutely true! A collaborator! A collaborator on the pre-Revolutionary press, and on the post-Revolutionary press. But somehow I missed out on the Revolutionary press. There were Reds here, Whites there, and Greens over yonder. There was the Crimea, the Underground, and so on. . . . So I had to become a shopkeeper. It really wasn't my own shop – it belonged to my father. Or, come to think of it, maybe it was my uncle. Me, I'm a factory worker by conviction. I've always said that it's better to die under the Red flag than starve to death in a ditch. With this slogan you can recruit a lot of intellectuals who think just like me. Excellency, give your orders! Our appetite is small.

PONT KICH

Ahem! Ahem!

MEZALYANSOVA

Pardon! My apologies! This is Mr. Pont Kich, a British Anglo-Saxon.

IVAN IVANOVICH

Have you been to England? *I've* been to England! Nothing but Englishmen everywhere! . . . Yes, I bought a cap in Liverpool, and I visited the house where Anti-Dühring[4] was born and lived. Most interesting! We must launch a broad campaign.

MEZALYANSOVA

Mr. Pont Kich is a famous philatelist – famous both in London and in the City. Being a philatelist – *ce qu'on appelle* "stamp collector" – he is tremendously interested in chemical plants, aviation, and art in general. He is a tremendously cultured and sociable man. He's even a Maecenas – *ce qu'on appelle* – how does one translate Maecenas, anyway? That is, in England he helps out film-makers and inventors. . . . You know, sort of like the Workers' and Peasants' Inspection,[5] only the other way around, *vous comprenez?* He's already had a view of Moscow from the top of the Izvestia skyscraper. ("Izvestia" in German is *Nachrichten*, by the way.) He's already been to see my friend the Commissar for Education,[6] and now he wants to see you. . . . Such a cultured and sociable gentleman! He even told us your address!

FOSKIN

He sure can smell things out, the nosy swine!

MEZALYANSOVA

Please, sir!

PONT KICH

Ouch! Ivan howled at the door, but the beasts were dining. Ouch! A mannequin went to Paradise, but a raccoon went to Hindustan. He put in too much pepper. Oh, the beasts! Invention.[7]

MEZALYANSOVA

Mr. Pont Kich says, in his own language, that all the people in his foggy homeland, from Ramsay MacDonald to Churchill, are as eager as so many ravenous beasts to find out about your invention. And he very humbly begs of you –

CHUDAKOV

But of course! Of course! My invention belongs to all mankind. I'll show him right now. . . . Very glad to do it. *(Moves to one side with* PONT KICH, *who has taken out a notebook, and begins to point out and explain this and that.)* Now here's the way this thing works. . . . Yes, that's right. And here we have two levers. And on the parallel crystal rulers. . . . Yes, that's right – in this direction. And here we have. . . . Yes, that's it. . . .

VELOSIPEDKIN *(taking* IVAN IVANOVICH *aside)*

Comrade, we have to help our friend Chudakov. I've been to all those offices where the signs read: "If you haven't been announced, don't come in!" I've hung around for hours at those places where "the case is closed," and so on. And I've practically spent the whole night under signs saying: "If the man you've come to see is busy, go away!" I've done all these things, and nothing has come of it. A very great invention may never see the light of day, just because of red tape – and because they're afraid to appropriate a hundred rubles or so. Comrade, with your influence, you must –

IVAN IVANOVICH

Yes, it's really frightful. You have to break eggs to make an omelet. I'll go straight to the Federal Bureau of Coordination. I'll go and see my friend Nikolay Ignatich right away. And if he refuses, I'll talk to Pavel Varfolomeyich in person. . . . Do you have a telephone here? Oh, you don't? Well, the slight defects in the mechanism. . . . Ah, what mechanisms they have in Switzerland! Have you ever been to Switzerland? *I've* been to Switzerland! Nothing but Swiss people everywhere! Most interesting!

PONT KICH *(puts his notebook in his pocket and shakes* CHUDAKOV*'s hand)*

Grandpa took a streetcar to Paradise, crawled from door to door, and didn't make it in a bad way. Blow, Ivan. Ten rubles?[8]

MEZALYANSOVA

Mr. Pont Kich says that if you need cash –

VELOSIPEDKIN

Cash? For Chudakov? He doesn't give a tinker's damn

for cash – he's got all he needs. I just went to the State Bank for him and came back with loads of cash. I've got so much it's disgusting. My pockets are jammed full, and it's chafing me. I've got twenty-ruble bills in this pocket, thirties in this one, and hundreds in these two. [*To* PONT KICH] All right! Good-bye! *(Shakes* PONT KICH's *hand, puts an arm around him, and enthusiastically shows him to the door.)*

MEZALYANSOVA

Please, I beg of you – be at least a *little* bit tactful! Those Young Communist League manners of yours will certainly cause a huge international conflict someday, if they haven't started one already. Good-bye! See you later.

IVAN IVANOVICH *(slapping* CHUDAKOV *on the shoulder and making ready to leave)*

Yes, when I was your age, I, too, was. . . . Well, you have to break eggs to make an omelet. We desperately need a Soviet Edison. *(From the doorway)* You don't have a telephone? Well, never mind, I'll be sure to tell my friend Nikander Piramidonovich.

MOMENTALNIKOV *(trotting after them and crooning)*

Excellency, give your orders! . . .

CHUDAKOV *(to* VELOSIPEDKIN)

I'm glad we've got some money.

VELOSIPEDKIN

We don't have any.

CHUDAKOV

What do you mean, we don't have any? If we don't, why were you bragging and saying we did? And worst of all, why did you turn down a solid offer from that foreigner?

VELOSIPEDKIN

You may be a genius, but you're still an idiot! Do you want to see your idea embodied in iron and come flying toward us from England in the form of a transparent aerial battleship in control of time – one that will invisibly attack our plants and our soviets?

CHUDAKOV

You're right! Why did I ever tell him all those things? And he wrote it all down in his notebook! But what about you? Why didn't you stop me? And besides, you yourself showed him to the door, and even put your arm around him.

VELOSIPEDKIN

Don't be silly. I had a good reason for putting my arm around him. My experience as a homeless child on the streets came in handy. It wasn't him I was embracing, but his pocket. Here it is – that English notebook! The Englishman lost his notebook.

CHUDAKOV

Bravo! Bravo! But what about the money?

VELOSIPEDKIN

Don't worry, I'll take care of everything. I'll gnaw through people's throats and swallow their Adam's apples! I won't just break eggs – I'll break heads! I've been trying to convince that character Optimistenko. I've roared at him. He's as smooth and polished as a ball bearing. His shiny surface reflects nothing but his boss – and upside down, at that. As for that bookkeeper, Nochkin, I've just about got him debureaucratized. But what can we possibly do with that bastard Pobedonosikov? He simply flattens all opposition with his seniority and his distinguished service record. Do you know his personal history? On the questionnaires, in the place where they ask: "What did you do before 1917?" he always puts: "I was in the Party." But nobody knows *which* party. Nobody knows whether it was the Bolsheviks or the Mensheviks, or maybe neither one nor the other. And there's something else. He escaped from prison by throwing tobacco in the guard's eyes. But today, twenty-five years later, time itself has filled his own eyes with the loose tobacco of petty details and minutes, and they are watering with smugness and joviality. With eyes like that, what can he possibly see? Socialism? Not at all! Only his inkwell and his paperweight!

FOSKIN

Comrades, what am I supposed to use for soldering – my own spit? And we need two more men here. It'll cost two hundred sixty rubles minimaximum.

POLYA *(rushes in, waving a package)*

Money! It's funny!

VELOSIPEDKIN *(to* FOSKIN, *handing him the money as the latter starts for the door on the run)*

Hurry up and grab a taxi! Round up some helpers and the stuff you need, and then come right back! *(To* POLYA*)* Well, how did you manage it? Did you persuade the chief through family channels?

POLYA

You think it's that simple – dealing with him? That's a laugh! Every time he comes home pregnant with resolutions, he hisses like a paper boa constrictor. It's not funny. You know that little old bookkeeper of his – that Nochkin? Well, I'd never seen him before. But today, on his lunch break, he came to me on the run and slipped me a package. "Pass it on," he told me, "and mum's the word!" It makes me laugh. Then he said, "I can't take it to them myself. I might be suspected of sympathizing." It's not funny.

CHUDAKOV

Maybe that money is –

VELOSIPEDKIN

Yes, that's something to think about. It strikes me as a bit odd. . . . But never mind. It doesn't matter. We'll look into it tomorrow.

(Enter FOSKIN, DVOYKIN, *and* TROYKIN.*)*

VELOSIPEDKIN

Everything ready?

FOSKIN

Ready!

VELOSIPEDKIN *(pulling them all together into a huddle)*

Come on, boys! Let's get going!

CHUDAKOV

Fine, that's just fine. The wiring is all soldered, the insulated compartments are in order, and the voltage has been checked. It looks as though we can go ahead. For the first time in the history of mankind. . . . Stand back! I'm switching it on. One, two, *three!*

(An explosion, with vivid blue light and smoke. They all draw back with a start, then rush forward to the site of the explosion. CHUDAKOV *retrieves a scrap of transparent, glass-like paper*

with rough, crumpled edges, getting his fingers burned in the process.)

Hurray! Let's shout and leap for joy! Just look at *this!* It's a letter – a letter written fifty years in the future. Do you understand? *In the future!* What an extraordinary style! Here, read it yourself! [*Gives paper to* VELOSIPEDKIN.]

VELOSIPEDKIN

What's there to read? "R-V-1-3-2-24-20." What's that, the telephone number of somebody named Comrade Arvey?

CHUDAKOV

It's not just the letters *r* and *v*, it's "arrive." They write in consonants only, which means a saving of twenty-five percent on the alphabet. The numbers 1, 3, and 2 show the sequence of the vowels: A, E, I, O, U: "arrive." See? The figure 24 means the 24th day of the month – tomorrow. And 20 indicates the hour. He, she, or it will arrive at eight o'clock tomorrow night. Or has there been a catastrophe? Do you see this burned, ragged edge of the letter? It means that somewhere along the course of time an obstacle, a body of some sort, was encountered in one of the fifty years occupying the space that is now empty. Hence the explosion. If we are to prevent the destruction of whoever or whatever is coming from there, we must immediately get more people and more money – a lot of both! We must immediately move the experiment up to the highest possible level – to the emptiest space. And if they don't help me, I'll hoist this machine up with my own back. But one way or another, everything will be settled tomorrow. Comrades, are you with me?

(They rush to the door.)

VELOSIPEDKIN

Let's go, boys! We'll grab 'em by the collar and make 'em come around. I'm going to gobble up some officials and spit out the buttons!

(The door is flung open from the outside.)

CHAIRMAN OF THE TENANTS' COMMITTEE

This is the last time I'm telling you! Clear out of here, and take your private shop[9] along with you! Your stink offends the nostrils of our important upstairs tenant,

Comrade Pobedonosikov. (*Notices* POLYA.) Oh! . . . Are—are you here, too? I just wanted to say, God bless your public-spirited work! And, oh, yes. I've been saving a marvelous electric fan for you. Good-bye now.

CURTAIN

ACT II

One side of a waiting room outside the office of Comrade POBEDONOSIKOV, *Chief, Federal Bureau of Coordination. To the right, a door with an illuminated sign reading:* IF YOU HAVEN'T BEEN ANNOUNCED, DON'T COME IN! *Behind a desk by the door,* OPTIMISTENKO *is receiving a long line of* PETITIONERS, *extending along the entire length of the wall. The* PETITIONERS *imitate one another's movements like so many cards being shuffled. When the wall is lighted from within, one sees only* POBEDONOSIKOV*'s office, with the silhouettes of the* PETITIONERS *in the foreground.*

OPTIMISTENKO

What's your problem, citizen?

FIRST PETITIONER

Please, Comrade Secretary, tie up! Please tie up!

OPTIMISTENKO

That can be arranged. Coordinating and tying in – both can be arranged. Did you receive an official notice?

FIRST PETITIONER

Notice? I gave him notice a long time ago, but it doesn't do any good. I can't make any headway. He just raises hell and fights back.

OPTIMISTENKO

But who is it that won't let you make headway with your problem?

FIRST PETITIONER

It's not a problem – it's Pashka Tigrolapov.[1]

OPTIMISTENKO

I'm sorry, citizen, but how could I possibly tie in this Pashka person?

FIRST PETITIONER

You're right! One man alone could never tie him up. But if you gave the order, two or three men could tie him up good! Please, comrade, tie up that hooligan! Everybody in the building is complaining about him.

OPTIMISTENKO

Damn it all! Why must you bother a big government agency with such trifles? Go to the police. . . . And you, Madame Citizen, what do you want?

WOMAN PETITIONER

Coordinate, your honor! Coordinate!

OPTIMISTENKO

That can be arranged. Both coordinating and tying in can be arranged. Every problem can be both coordinated and tied in. Has there been an official commitment?

WOMAN PETITIONER

No, your honor, I can't have him committed. At the police station they said yes, they could commit him for a week. But then, your honor, how would I eat? Besides, once he got out he'd just start beating me again.

OPTIMISTENKO

I'm sorry, Madame Citizen, but you stated you needed to have something coordinated. Why give me a long story about your husband?

WOMAN PETITIONER

Because, your honor, it's me and my husband that have to be coordinated. It's very uncoordinated, the way we live. He's a very profound drinker. And they're all afraid to lay a finger on him because he's in the Party.

OPTIMISTENKO

Damn it all! Now you just listen to me! I don't want to see you around here again pestering a big government agency with your petty problems. We can't be bothered with trifles. The government is interested in big things: various kinds of Fordism, other speedup systems, and so on.

(CHUDAKOV *and* VELOSIPEDKIN *rush in.*)

Ah! And just where do you think *you're* going?

VELOSIPEDKIN *(trying to elbow* OPTIMISTENKO *aside)*

We have to see Comrade Pobedonosikov immediately.

It's urgent!

CHUDAKOV

Immediately. It's urgent!

OPTIMISTENKO

Aha! Now I recognize you! Is it you yourself, or your brother? There was a young man who used to come here –

CHUDAKOV

That was me.

OPTIMISTENKO

No, it wasn't. He didn't have a beard.

CHUDAKOV

I didn't even have a mustache when I first started knocking at your door. Comrade, this can't go on! We're here to see Pobedonosikov himself. We have to see Fedburoco in person.

OPTIMISTENKO

There's no necessity for that. There's no need for you to bother him. I myself in person can give you full satisfaction. Everything is in order. A final decision has been made in your case.

CHUDAKOV *(echoing his words joyfully)*

Full satisfaction, you say?

VELOSIPEDKIN *(echoing his words joyfully)*

A final decision, you say? You mean we've broken through the bureaucrats? *Really?* That's wonderful!

OPTIMISTENKO

What on earth are you talking about, comrades? How could there possibly be any bureaucrats or red tape around here just before a housecleaning? Now. With this new card-file system, I have no need to sort through any papers. I have everything right here at my fingertips. First, I find the drawer with your file in it. Next, I take out your file. And then I hold in my hands the final decision. Yes, here it is.

(They all peer at it.)

As I already told you, it's the final decision: "Rejected."

(The upstage lights dim out, and the scene shifts to the interior of POBEDONOSIKOV*'s office.)*

POBEDONOSIKOV *(leafing through documents while trying to*

ring up a party on the telephone and, when not cranking the phone, pacing back and forth, dictating)

"And so, comrades, that little streetcar bell – an alarm bell, a revolutionary bell, a bell summoning all to come – must ring out like a big churchbell in the heart of every worker and peasant. For today the Lenin Streetcar Line is linking that former stronghold of the bourgeoisie, the Haymarket, with the public square now known as the Tenth Anniversary of Soviet Medicine Square. . . ." *(On the telephone)* Hello! Hello! *(Dictating again)* "Before the Revolution, who rode on that streetcar line? Has-been intellectuals, priests, and the upper class. How much did they pay? They paid five kopecks per stop. What did they ride in? In a yellow streetcar. And who will be riding on that line now? We, the workers of the entire universe, will ride on it. How will we ride? We will ride with all Soviet conveniences, in a *red* streetcar. And how much will we pay? Only ten kopecks. And so, comrades. . . ." *(The telephone rings; he talks into it.)* Yes, yes, yes. None at all? [*To the* TYPIST] Where did we stop?

TYPIST

We stopped on: "And so, comrades. . . ."

POBEDONOSIKOV

Oh, yes. "And so, comrades, remember that Leo Tolstoy was a very great and never-to-be-forgotten wielder of the pen. On the borderline between two worlds, his heritage of the past shines brilliantly at us like a great star of art, like an entire constellation, like the greatest of the great constellations – the Great Bear. Leo Tolstoy – "

TYPIST

Pardon me, comrade. Before, you were talking about a streetcar, and now for some reason you've put Leo Tolstoy in it while it's moving along. As far as I can see, that's some kind of violation of the literary and streetcar regulations.

POBEDONOSIKOV

What? What streetcar? Oh, yes! All these continual greetings and speeches! . . . But you will please refrain from comment during working hours. If you have any self-criticisms[2] to make, you can always use the bulletin-board newspaper. That's what it's for. Now let's go on. . . . "Even Leo Tolstoy, even that greatest bear of the pen, if he could take a look at our achievements in the form of the above-mentioned streetcar – even he would affirm in the face of world imperialism: 'I cannot remain silent. Just look at them – the red fruits of general and compulsory education!'[3] And in these days when we are celebrating–" [*Breaks off.*] It's scandalous! A nightmare! Tell that bookkeeper, Comrade Nochkin – or rather, Citizen Nochkin – to come in here immediately!

(The lights in POBEDONOSIKOV*'s office dim out. Once again we see the queue outside the office.* CHUDAKOV *and* VELOSIPEDKIN *are trying to break through into the office.)*

VELOSIPEDKIN

Comrade Optimistenko, this is insulting!

OPTIMISTENKO

Not at all. There's no insult involved. You heard what the decision was: "Rejected." Your invention doesn't fit into the overall plan for the next quarter.

VELOSIPEDKIN

But socialism isn't being built just in your next quarter!

OPTIMISTENKO

Don't you dare interfere in our governmental functions with those fantasies of yours! *(To* BELVEDONSKY, *who has just entered)* Glad to see you here! Make yourself at home. *(To* CHUDAKOV*)* Your invention is not coordinated with the Commissariat of Transportation, and is not required by the broad masses of workers and peasants.

VELOSIPEDKIN

What does the Commissariat of Transportation have to do with it? Such stupidity!

CHUDAKOV

Naturally, we can't foresee all the great consequences. But it is quite possible that eventually my machine can be usefully applied to problems of transportation – at a maximum speed and almost outside of time.

VELOSIPEDKIN

For that matter, it can even be coordinated with the Commissariat of Transportation. For example, you get into your seat at three o'clock in the morning, and by five o'clock you're already in Leningrad.

OPTIMISTENKO

See? What did I tell you? Proposal rejected – it's not practical. What's the use of being in Leningrad at five in the morning? There's not a single government agency open at that hour. *(The red light on the telephone starts flashing. He listens, then shouts)* Have Nochkin report to Comrade Pobedonosikov!

(Dodging CHUDAKOV *and* VELOSIPEDKIN, *who rush in his direction,* NOCHKIN *trots in to see* POBEDONOSIKOV; *the scene shifts to the latter's office.)*

POBEDONOSIKOV *(cranking the telephone and wheezing into it)*

Damn it all! Hello, Ivan Nikanorich? I want you to get me two tickets. Yes, yes, on the international line. *What?* You're not in charge any more? Damn it! I need two tickets but don't know who to call to get them. With this work load a man simply loses all contact with the masses! Hello! Hello! *(To the* TYPIST*)* Where did we stop?

TYPIST

On "And so, comrades. . . ."

POBEDONOSIKOV

"And so, comrades, Alexander Semyonich Pushkin, the peerless author of both the opera *Eugene Onegin* and the play of the same name – "[4]

TYPIST

Pardon me, comrade, but first you got a streetcar going, then you put Tolstoy in it, and now Pushkin has climbed on. But the streetcar hasn't even made one stop yet.

POBEDONOSIKOV

What Tolstoy? What does a streetcar have to do with it? Oh, yes! All those continual speeches and greetings! But I must ask you to refrain from making objections. Here I am, working away with great consistency and perfectionism, pursuing a single theme without in any way digressing, while you . . . you. . . . For that matter, Tolstoy and Pushkin – and even Byron, if you like – may have been born at different times, but we're still going to celebrate their birthdays all together, and in common. . . . You know, I'm thinking of writing just one general article as a guide. Then you could break it down into individual subjects, avoiding all distortions of self-criticism – provided that in general you keep to your place. But in general you think more about putting on lipstick and powder, and there's no place for you in my agency. I should have overhauled my secretariat a long time ago and brought in some teen-age girls from the Young Communist League. As of today I must request that you –

(*Enter* BELVEDONSKY.)

Greetings, comrade! Mission accomplished? With all possible speed?

BELVEDONSKY

Mission accomplished – naturally. I hardly got a wink of sleep, so to speak, being in socialist competition with myself, but I accomplished everything in accordance with the social job order and the advance to the extent of the full three hundred percent. Would you care, comrade, to gaze upon your future piece of furniture?

POBEDONOSIKOV

Demonstrate it!

BELVEDONSKY

With pleasure! You of course know and can see, as the famous historian said, that there are various Looey styles. For instance, there's Looey the Fourteenth, so-called by the French after the Revolution of 1848 because he came directly after Looey the Thirteenth. Then there's Looey Jacob.[5] And finally, I take the liberty of recommending to you, as the most perfect, Looey Mauvais Goût.

POBEDONOSIKOV

The styles are OK, they're well selected. But what about the price?

BELVEDONSKY

All three Looeys are about the same price.

POBEDONOSIKOV

In that case I think I'll take Looey the Fourteenth. But naturally, in accordance with the order on cost reduction issued by the Workers' and Peasants' Inspection, I must suggest that you proceed with all possible speed to straighten out the legs of the chairs and sofas, remove the gilt, paint them over so they look like fumed oak, and put on a few Soviet national emblems here and there – on the backs of the chairs and in other prominent places.

BELVEDONSKY

Exquisite! There were more than fifteen Looeys, and none of them could think up anything like that! But you did it right away, in the Bolshevik style – in the Revolutionary style! Comrade, allow me to continue with your portrait and immortalize you as an executive of the innovator type – and also as a distributor of loans. *Prison and Exile* is crying out for you. (I mean the magazine of that name, of course.) And the Museum of the Revolution is crying out for you. We can send the original there; they'd give anything to get it. As for the prints, your grateful employees can buy them on the installment plan, with deductions from their pay checks. Do I have your permission to proceed?

POBEDONOSIKOV

By no means! I couldn't think of absenting myself from the helm of command for such a trivial matter. But on the other hand, if the portrait is necessary for completeness of the historical record, and if it won't interrupt my work, I'll be glad to oblige. I'll sit right here behind my desk. But I want you to paint me retrospectively, as if I were on horseback.

BELVEDONSKY

I've already sketched your horse at my studio, from memory, taking my inspiration from the race tracks. Also, believe it or not, to get certain details right I looked at myself in the mirror. All I have to do now is put you and the horse together. Allow me to move that waste-paper basket to one side. Ah, what modesty in a man who has performed such distinguished services. Now if you'll just straighten out the line of your heroic leg a little. . . . How that polished boot does shine! Makes a man want to lick it! Yes, only in the work of Michelangelo does one find such a clean line! Do you know Michelangelo?

POBEDONOSIKOV

Angelov? An Armenian?

BELVEDONSKY

No, Italian.

POBEDONOSIKOV

A Fascist?

BELVEDONSKY

Really, now!

POBEDONOSIKOV

I don't know him.

BELVEDONSKY

You *don't?*

POBEDONOSIKOV

Does he know me?

BELVEDONSKY

I don't know. . . . He's an artist, too.

POBEDONOSIKOV

Ah! Well, he probably knows me. After all, there's lots of artists, but only one Fedburoco.

BELVEDONSKY

My pencil is trembling. How can I convey the dialectics of your character with a sense of common, everyday modesty? Your self-esteem, comrade, is titanic! Now, just let your eyes flash over your right shoulder and above your fountain pen. Allow me to immortalize this moment!

[*A knock at the door*]

POBEDONOSIKOV

Come in!

(NOCHKIN *enters.)*

You?

NOCHKIN

I –

POBEDONOSIKOV

Two hundred and thirty?

NOCHKIN

Two hundred and forty.

POBEDONOSIKOV

Did you drink it up?

NOCHKIN

I lost it playing cards.

POBEDONOSIKOV

Monstrous! Incomprehensible! Who? An embezzler!

Where? In my agency! When? When I am leading my agency toward socialism in the great footsteps of the great Karl Marx, and in conformity to instructions from the top—

NOCHKIN

Well, after all, Karl Marx used to play cards, too.

POBEDONOSIKOV

Karl Marx? Cards? Never!

NOCHKIN

OK, never. But what did Franz Mehring write on the subject? What did he say on page seventy-two of his major work, *Karl Marx in Private Life*? Marx played cards! Our great teacher played cards.

POBEDONOSIKOV

Naturally, I have read Mehring. In the first place, he exaggerates. In the second place, Karl Marx did in fact play cards, but it was games of skill, not of pure chance.

NOCHKIN

Maybe so. But his classmate and contemporary, the famous Ludwig Feuerbach, who was an expert, wrote that Marx also played games of chance.

POBEDONOSIKOV

Well, yes, naturally I've read Comrade Feuerbach. Karl Marx sometimes played games of chance, but not with money.

NOCHKIN

Oh, yes. With money.

POBEDONOSIKOV

But he used his own money, not the government's.

NOCHKIN

I always thought that everybody who had studied Marx knew there was one memorable occasion when he gambled with government funds.

POBEDONOSIKOV

Naturally, that historic case obliges us, in view of the historical precedent, to take a more cautious approach toward your misdemeanor. But still —

NOCHKIN

Oh, stop going around in circles! Karl Marx never played cards in his life! But what's the use of talking to you? Could you ever really understand a human being?

All you care about is following precedents and paragraphs, you old stuffed briefcase! You paper clip!

POBEDONOSIKOV

What's this? *Insults?* And not only to me, your immediate, responsible superior, but also to the mediocre – no, what am I saying?—the irresponsible shade of Karl Marx![6] You'll never get away with it! I'll have you arrested!

NOCHKIN

Don't trouble yourself with a phone call, comrade. I'll inform the Moscow DA's office myself.

POBEDONOSIKOV

I won't have it! I won't let you!

BELVEDONSKY

Just a moment, comrade. Please hold that pose. Allow me to immortalize this great moment!

TYPIST

Ha, ha, ha!

POBEDONOSIKOV

So! You're taking sides with an embezzler, eh? You're laughing, are you? And with painted lips to boot! *Out! (Alone, cranking the telephone)* Hello? Hello? Damn it all, who's speaking? Alexander Petrovich? Listen, I've been trying to get you for three days. What? The heat is off? Congratulations! Yes, of course, of course! How could there be any doubt about it? . . . As usual – busy all day and all night. . . . Yes, today, finally. Two tickets, first class. With a stenographer. What does the Board of Inspection have to do with it? I have to finish dictating a report. So it's two hundred forty rubles for a round trip – what difference does that make? We can get it approved as per diem expenses, or some such thing. Yes, with all possible speed, by messenger. . . . Yes, of course I'll put it through for you. . . . That's right. To me, at Cape Green. . . . Well, good-bye now, and please accept my comradely best wishes. *(Throws the telephone receiver back on the hook, and starts singing to the tune of Bizet's "Toreador Song")* Hello, hello!

(The waiting room. CHUDAKOV *and* VELOSIPEDKIN *make a dash for* POBEDONOSIKOV'S *office.)*

OPTIMISTENKO

Just where do you think you're going? I must ask you to have some respect for the labors and activities of government personnel!

(Enter MEZALYANSOVA. CHUDAKOV *and* VELOSIPEDKIN *make another lunge.)*

No, no. . . . *(Takes* MEZALYANSOVA'S *arm in his; in a tone of reproach)* You must bypass the waiting line, in accordance with the telephonogram. . . . Everything is ready. . . . Why, *I* did it! I told him – letting the words sink in, you know – that his spouse was running around with Young Communist Leaguers. Initially, he was furious. He said, "I will not tolerate unbridled flirtation in the case of persons lacking proper seniority and status." But later on he was even glad of it. He's already fired his secretary for unethical use of lipstick. . . . Go right on in! It's all right.

And under every leaflet,
There was a place for her. . . .[7]

(MEZALYANSOVA *exits to* POBEDONOSIKOV'S *office.)*

CHUDAKOV

So now you've let *her* go in! Comrade, you must understand me! No power on earth – neither the power of science nor that of the Devil himself – can stop what is about to happen! If we can't shift our experiment to the space above the city, there may even be an explosion.

OPTIMISTENKO

An *explosion?* That's enough of that! Don't you dare threaten a government agency! It's not proper to get us all worked up and nervous! And if there *is* an explosion, we'll report you to Certain Competent Authorities.

VELOSIPEDKIN

Get this through your head, stupid! *You're* the one that ought to be reported to Certain Authorities, competent or incompetent. Everywhere in the working world, people are burning to get on with the job. But you, you blind gut, all you do is piss on them with your bureaucratic palaver!

OPTIMISTENKO

You will kindly refrain from personal attacks! The individual has no special role in history. We're not living in the time of the tsars. Before, there was a need for enthusiasm. But now we have historical materialism, and nobody needs your enthusiasm.

(Enter MEZALYANSOVA.*)*

Citizens, you can leave now. No more interviews today.

MEZALYANSOVA *(carrying a briefcase; singing)*

When I gaze at thy beauty, O bayadère!
Tra-la-la-la, tra-la-la-la. . . .

CURTAIN

ACT III

The stage represents an extension of the orchestra seats. There are several empty seats in the first row. A signal: "We are beginning." The audience looks at the stage through opera glasses, and the [*actors on*] *stage looks back at the audience through opera glasses. People begin to whistle and stamp their feet as they shout, "Time to start!"*

DIRECTOR

Comrades, don't get all worked up! Owing to circumstances beyond our control, we've had to delay the third act for a few minutes.

(A pause; then more shouts of "Time to start!")

Just another minute, comrades. *(Aside)* Well, are they coming? This kind of delay is embarrassing. After all, the discussion could wait until the play is over. Go find them in the lobby and drop a polite hint. Ah! Here they come! Make yourselves at home, comrades. Why, no, of course not! Glad to have you. No, a minute or two doesn't matter – not even a half hour. This isn't a train we're running here. We can always hold things up for a while. Everybody understands the kind of times we're living in. Why, you people may have been discussing all kinds of government matters – even planetary matters. Did you see the first two acts? Well, how did you like them? Naturally, we're all interested in your impressions and, generally speaking, in the views of –

POBEDONOSIKOV

It's not bad – not bad at all. I was just telling Ivan Ivanovich. It makes some clever points – brings things out very sharply. But still and all, it's not quite what it should be.

DIRECTOR

But we can correct all that. We always try to improve. If you'll just name something specific, why then, of course, before you can say "Jack Robinson," we'll –

POBEDONOSIKOV

It's all laid on too thick. Life isn't like that. . . . Take, for instance, that Pobedonosikov. Whatever you say, it's unseemly. From all the evidence, he's supposed to be a comrade with an important position. Yet he's presented in a bad light, and then for some reason he's called "Fedburoco." We don't have officials like that. It's unnatural. Not lifelike. Not the way things are. You'll have to rewrite that part – tone it down, poeticize it, soften the contours. . . .

IVAN IVANOVICH

He's right. It's unseemly. Do you have a telephone here? I'll call my friend Fyodor Fyodorovich. He'll take care of it, naturally. . . . Oh, would that be inconvenient during the performance? All right, I'll do it later. Comrade Momentalnikov, we must launch a broad campaign.

MOMENTALNIKOV

Excellency, give your orders!
Our appetite is small.
Just say the word – one little word! –
And we'll revile them, one and all!

DIRECTOR

Hold on there, comrades! After all, this performance comes under the head of public self-criticism. And we have the censor's permission to present, by way of exception, a negative literary character.

POBEDONOSIKOV

What's that you said? A "character"? What makes you think you can say such a thing about a top government executive? A thing like that may be said only about some good-for-nothing who's not a Party member. A "character" indeed! Pobedonosikov isn't a "character," he's Fedburoco – appointed, moreover, by the top policy organs. And you call him a "character"! For that matter, if his behavior involves any contraindicated violations, they should be reported to the competent authorities for investigation.

And finally, when the facts have been checked by the Federal Prosecutor's Office and published by the Inspection Board, they should be converted into symbolic images. *That* I would understand. But when you put him on stage to be laughed at by the general public –

DIRECTOR

Comrade, you are quite right. But it fits in with the action of the play.

POBEDONOSIKOV

Action? What action? There is no action you can possibly take. Your job is to point things out. As for action, don't worry! The competent Party and soviet agencies will do very well without you. Besides, you should also point out the bright side of our work. You should pick something exemplary. My agency, for instance. Or myself, for example.

IVAN IVANOVICH

He's absolutely right! You should go and visit his agency! You'll see directives being carried out, circulars being circulated, efficiency measures being implemented, and papers that have been lying there for years in perfect order. There's a conveyor belt for applications, complaints, and memoranda. It's a regular little nook of socialism. Most interesting!

DIRECTOR

But, comrades, allow me –

POBEDONOSIKOV

I won't allow you! I have no right to. And I'm amazed that in general you were allowed to do this at all. Why, it even discredits us in the eyes of Europe. *(To* MEZALYANSOVA*)* Don't interpret that remark, please.[1]

MEZALYANSOVA

Oh, of course not! It's all right. He had some caviar at a banquet a little while ago, and now he's drowsy.

POBEDONOSIKOV

And what kind of person are you setting off against me? An inventor? But what did he invent? The Westinghouse brake? Did he think up the fountain pen? Do streetcars have to walk if he's not around? Did he officize a ration?[2]

DIRECTOR

I beg your pardon?

POBEDONOSIKOV

I say, did he rationalize an office? No! So what does all this amount to? We don't need dreamers. Socialism is a matter of bookkeeping.

IVAN IVANOVICH

Have you ever been in a bookkeeping department? *I've* been in a bookkeeping department. Nothing but numbers everywhere! Big numbers, little numbers, all different kinds of numbers. And in the end they all match up. That's bookkeeping! Most interesting!

DIRECTOR

Comrades, don't get us wrong. We may make mistakes; but our idea was to put the theater into the service of the struggle and positive action. People look, and they get to work. They look, and they are aroused. They look, and they expose whatever is bad.

POBEDONOSIKOV

For my part, I'm asking you, in the name of all workers and peasants, not to arouse *me!* Think it over, you alarm clock! Instead of arousing me, you should create pleasant sights and sounds for my eyes and ears.

MEZALYANSOVA

That's right – pleasant sights and sounds. . . .

POBEDONOSIKOV

After our governmental and public-spirited activity, we like to relax. You must go back to the classics! You must learn from the great geniuses of the damnable past! How many times do I have to tell you? Remember how the poet sang:

After all those conferences,
We feel neither joy nor grief;
We hope for nothing from the future,
We *dum-dee-dum dee-dum* regrets.[3]

MEZALYANSOVA

Yes, of course art must reflect life – the beautiful lives of beautiful, live people. Show us beautiful lively creatures against beautiful landscapes, and bourgeois decadence in general. In fact, if it's necessary for propaganda, you could even show us a belly dance. Or you could let us see, for instance, how the new struggle against the old way of life is being waged in the putrefied Western world. You could use the stage to show us, for example, that in Paris they don't have an Organization for Political Work Among Women – they have the foxtrot instead. Or we could see the new skirt styles they are wearing in that old, decrepit society – *ce qu'on appelle le beau monde.* Do you follow me?

IVAN IVANOVICH

That's it! Make it pretty for us! At the Bolshoi Theater they always make it pretty for us. Did you see *The Red Poppy?* I saw *The Red Poppy.* Most interesting! Everywhere you looked, they were dancing, and singing, and flitting about – all those different elves and . . . syphilids.

DIRECTOR

You mean sylphides?

IVAN IVANOVICH

Oh, yes, of course. Sylphides. Very observant of you. We must launch a broad campaign. Oh, yes indeed! All kinds of different elves and twelves. . . .[4] Most interesting!

DIRECTOR

Pardon my saying so, but we've already had a lot of elves, and their further multiplication was not provided for in the five-year plan. Besides, the action of the play doesn't call for them. But as for relaxation, I see what you mean, of course. So we'll make the necessary changes in the play, introducing cheerful and graceful supplementary scenes. Take our so-called Comrade Pobedonosikov, for instance. If we give him some rib-tickling material, even he can make everyone laugh. I'll give him a few pointers right now, and the role will simply shine like a diamond. Comrade, just pick up any three or four objects – let's say, a pen, your signature, a sheet of paper, and your maximum salary[5] – and go through a few juggling tricks. Toss up the pen, catch the paper, sign it, and take the maximum salary. Catch the pen, take the paper, sign it, and grab the maximum salary. One, two, three, four! One, two, three four!

This is the way
We spend the day –
We bu-reau-crats.

This is the way
We spend the day –
We bu-reau-crats.[6]

Does that get to you?

POBEDONOSIKOV *(enthusiastically)*

That's fine! Cheers you up! Nothing decadent about it, and it doesn't offend anybody or anything! Besides, it's great for training.

MEZALYANSOVA

Oui, c'est très pédagogique.

POBEDONOSIKOV

Agility in bodily movements is morally uplifting to anyone just beginning a career. This exercise is simple and easy to understand. Even children could be brought to see it. And just between you and me, the new class – the working class – is an overgrown child. Of course, this act is still rather angular. It lacks those rounded lines, that juiciness –

DIRECTOR

Well, if you like it, it offers unlimited horizons for fantasy. We can present a directly symbolical picture, using all available actors. *(Claps his hands.)* All men out on stage! Everybody down on one knee! Now bend down low and look enslaved. With an invisible pickax in your visible hand, dig away at invisible coal. More gloom on your faces, please! Dark forces are evilly oppressing you! Good! That's the way!

You there, you'll play the role of Capital. Over here, Comrade Capital! Now dance over all the others with an expression of class domination. Embrace an imaginary woman with an invisible arm, and drink imaginary champagne. Fine! Very good! Keep it up

All available female personnel – out on stage! You, there, you're Miss Liberty – you seem to have the right attitude for it. And you're Miss Equality, because it's all the same to me whoever plays the part. And you're Miss

Fraternity, because brotherly feelings are about all you'll ever arouse in anybody.

Get ready now, and let's go! Stir up the imaginary masses with an imaginary call to action! Infect them! Infect them all with your enthusiasm! What do you think you're doing there? Raise your leg higher, simulating an economic upswing. Capital, dance off to the left; try to look like the Second International. Why are you waving your arms like that? Stick out your imperialist tentacles! ... What, you don't have any tentacles? Then you shouldn't have got into acting. Well, stick out whatever you want to. Try to seduce the dancing ladies with imaginary wealth. Girls, reject him with a sharp movement of the left hand. There, that's it! Imaginary laboring masses, rise up in symbolic revolt. Comrade Capital, collapse gracefully. Very good!

Now, Capital, expire effectively. Give us some colorful spasms. Excellent!

All you men, throw off your imaginary fetters and rise up toward a symbolical sun! Miss Liberty, Miss Equality, and Miss Fraternity, simulate the firm advance of the workers' cohorts. Now place your would-be workers' feet on the would-be overthrown would-be Capital. Liberty, Equality, and Fraternity – smile as though you were filled with joy.

Men, pretend you are "those who were nothing" and imagine you are "those who shall become all."[7] Climb up on each other's shoulders, symbolizing the growth of socialist competition. Good! Now build a pyramid with your would-be powerful bodies, personifying in plastic form a symbol of communism. Take an imaginary hammer in your free hand and swing it to the tempo of a free country, conveying the emotion of the struggle. Orchestra, add an industrial din to the music! Good! That's it!

All women out on stage! Hang imaginary garlands around the necks of the workers in the great universal army of labor. That's to symbolize the blooming of the flowers of happiness under socialism.

Good! Now, if you will be so kind. Ready? A relaxing little pantomime on the theme:

The actors have all had their fill
Of Labor and of Capital.

POBEDONOSIKOV

Bravo! Splendid! When you have a talent like that, how can you squander it on topical trifles – on frothy tabloid satire? What we just saw is real art. It makes sense to me, to Ivan Ivanovich, and to the masses.

IVAN IVANOVICH

That's right! Do you have a telephone here? I'll call. . . . Well, I'll call somebody, because my soul is simply overflowing! That was so infectious! Comrade Momentalnikov, we must launch a broad campaign.

MOMENTALNIKOV

Excellency, give your orders!
Our appetite is small.
Just give us bread and circuses –
We'll cheer for anything at all.

POBEDONOSIKOV

Yes, it's very good! It has everything. All it needs is a character symbolizing self-criticism – that's very timely right now. Just put a little desk in one corner, and let him write articles while you go on with your own business. Thanks, and good-bye now. After such an elegant finale, I don't want my impressions dulled, or their bloom rubbed off. Please accept my comradely best wishes!

IVAN IVANOVICH

Pleace accept my comradely best wishes! By the way, what's the name of that little actress there – the third from the end? She has a very pretty talent on her. Looks delicious. . . . We must launch a broad campaign – or maybe even a narrow one. . . . Just the two of us, I mean. I'll give her a call. Or maybe she'd better call me.

MOMENTALNIKOV

Excellency, give your orders!
My modesty is slight.
Just give me her number,
I'll call her up tonight.

(Two USHERS *stop* VELOSIPEDKIN, *who is trying to get into the first row of seats.)*

USHER

Hey, citizen! You, there! Where do you think you're going? You are politely requested to scram!

VELOSIPEDKIN

I have to get into the first row.

USHER

Maybe you'd like some free refreshments, too, eh? Citizen, you are being requested politely – Do you hear me? Your ticket is for the workers' section. Why are you butting in here? These seats are for high-class people.

VELOSIPEDKIN

I have to get into the first row to see Comrade Pobedonosikov on business.

USHER

Now look here, citizen! People come to the theater for pleasure, not for business. You are politely requested to roll out of here like a salami!

VELOSIPEDKIN

Pleasure can wait till the day after tomorrow. My business is for today. If I have to, I'll turn all these seats upside down – not just the first row, but all of them, and the box seats to boot!

USHER

Citizen, you are politely requested to *get the hell out!* You didn't check your coat, you didn't buy a program, and you don't even have a ticket!

VELOSIPEDKIN

I didn't come here to see a play – I came on business. And my ticket is my Party card. . . . Comrade Pobedonosikov, it's you I came to see!

POBEDONOSIKOV

Why are you shouting? And who do you mean? Somebody named Pobedonosikov?

VELOSIPEDKIN

Let's cut out the joking and the playacting. You're Pobedonosikov, and I came to see you because you're Fedburoco in person.

POBEDONOSIKOV

Before addressing a responsible, high-sitting comrade,

you should at least know his last name – and preferably his first and middle names, too.

VELOSIPEDKIN

Well, since you're responsible, respond and tell me why the people in your agency are blocking Chudakov's invention. We have only a few minutes left. If we don't act now, the disaster will be irreparable. Give us some funds immediately, and we'll make the experiment at the highest altitude –

POBEDONOSIKOV

What kind of nonsense is this? What Chudakov? What altitude? In general, I myself am leaving today for the highest altitude in the Caucasus Mountains.

VELOSIPEDKIN

Chudakov is an inventor.

POBEDONOSIKOV

There's lots of inventors, but only one me. And in general I must ask you not to disturb me in those rare moments of relaxation scheduled for me by the proper authorities. Come to see me on Friday.

(The DIRECTOR *waves his hand frantically at* VELOSIPEDKIN.*)*

VELOSIPEDKIN

They'll come to see you – not on Friday, but tonight. And it won't be me. It'll be –

POBEDONOSIKOV

I don't care who comes. Anyway, they won't see me, they'll see my deputy. When my vacation has been authorized by official order, it means I'm not here. You must understand the construction of our Constitution. . . . This is scandalous!

VELOSIPEDKIN *(to* IVAN IVANOVICH*)*

Try to make him understand! Telephone it into his head! You promised, remember?

IVAN IVANOVICH

Pestering a man on vacation with business matters! Most interesting! Is there a telephone here? I'll call my friend Nikolay Alexandrovich. We must spare the health of our old executives while they're still young.

DIRECTOR

Comrade Velosipedkin, please don't make a scene! After all, he's not in the play – he just looks like the other guy. Please! I don't want them to catch on. You'll receive full satisfaction before the play is over.

POBEDONOSIKOV

Good-bye, comrade! All I can say is this. You call it r-r-revolutionary drama, and yet you yourself stir up – how did you put it? – arouse us executives. That's not for the masses. The workers and peasants won't understand it. It's a good thing they won't, too; and you mustn't explain it to them. Why are you turning us into characters – into actors? We want to be inactive – what do you call 'em – spectators. No, siree! Next time I'll go to another theater.

IVAN IVANOVICH

He's absolutely right! Did you see *The Squaring of the Cherry?* I saw *Uncle Turbines.*[8] Most interesting!

DIRECTOR *(to* VELOSIPEDKIN)

Just look what you've done! You almost wrecked the whole show! [*To the cast*] On stage, please! The play will continue.

CURTAIN

ACT IV

Within an apartment building: crisscrossing stairways, landings, doors of apartments. POBEDONOSIKOV, *carrying a suitcase, emerges onto the upper landing. He tries to push the door shut with his shoulder, but* POLYA *pulls it open and rushes out onto the landing, catching hold of the suitcase.*

POLYA

What's this? You mean you're really leaving me behind? It's not funny.

POBEDONOSIKOV

I must ask you to break off this conversation. Such a petty-bourgeois family scene! Every doctor says that for a completely restful vacation, one must get away from one's usual surroundings. And "one" means me, not you. So I'm on my way to regenerate an important government organism—to improve its health in various mountainous regions.

POLYA

You think I don't know what's going on? I noticed they brought you two tickets. So at first I thought. . . . But how – just how would I be in your way? It's ridiculous.

POBEDONOSIKOV

You'd better forget those petty-bourgeois notions of a vacation. I don't have time to go cruising around in some little boat. Such petty pleasures are for underlings. "Glide on, my gondola!" No gondola for me, thank you! I'm taking a government-owned ship. And I'm not going just to get a suntan! I always plan ahead for the current moment. And then, when I get there – a speech, a report, a resolution. In short, socialism. And in accordance with my official position, I'm entitled by law to a stenographer.

POLYA

When did I ever interfere with your stenography? That's a laugh! You can play the hypocrite with other people if you want to, but why try to fool me? Let me come along, too, for the love of God! You can stenograph all night if you want to, I don't care. It's ridiculous!

POBEDONOSIKOV

Shush! You'll compromise me with your disorganized outcries – especially when they're religious, like "For the love of God!" Shush! Kozlyakovsky lives downstairs, remember? He might tell Pavel Petrovich. And Pavel Petrovich is a friend of Semyon Afanasich.

POLYA

What's there to hide? You make me laugh!

POBEDONOSIKOV

You! You're the one that should hide things! You should hide those bourgeois, old-womanish bad moods of yours that have made our marriage so unequal! Just give it some thought – if only out of respect for Nature – that Nature whose beauties I shall view on my trip. Just think of it – you and I! There was a time when we used to go out on patrol together, and sleep under the same army coat. That was enough, then. But things are different now. I've come up the intellectual and professional ladder – and up the apartment-house stairway to a better place. You, too, should be able to educate yourself and learn to zigzag dialectically, like me. But what do I see in your face? Only vestiges of the past – the chains of the old way of life!

POLYA

Do I ever get in your way? It's ridiculous. You're the one who's turned *me* into a plucked setting hen!

POBEDONOSIKOV

Shush! Enough of your jealousy! Anyway, you yourself hang around some of the neighbors' apartments. The pleasures of the Young Communist League, eh? Did you think I didn't know? You couldn't even find yourself a boy friend appropriate to my social position! You hussy!

POLYA

Stop it! It's not funny.

POBEDONOSIKOV

I've already told you that Kozlyakovsky lives just downstairs. Let's go back inside. We'll have to finish this once and for all!

(He pushes POLYA *back into the apartment, and slams the door.* VELOSIPEDKIN *appears on the lower stairway, followed by* CHUDAKOV, *who is carrying an invisible machine, with the help of* DVOYKIN *and* TROYKIN.*)*

VELOSIPEDKIN

Come on, boys! Just another twenty steps or so. But keep it quiet. If he hears us coming, he'll hide behind his assistants and his papers again. We want him right there when this bomb of time explodes in his home.

CHUDAKOV

I'm afraid we won't make it. An error of one-tenth of a second means a whole hour by our time system.

DVOYKIN

Do you feel how the parts are heating up under our hands? The glass is almost melting.

TROYKIN

On my side the plating is getting awfully hot. It's like a stove! Honest, just like a stove! I'm having a hard time holding on without getting burned.

CHUDAKOV

The weight of the machine is increasing with each second. I could almost swear some foreign body is materializing inside it.

DVOYKIN

Comrade Chudakov, let's go faster. I can't stand it! We're carrying fire!

VELOSIPEDKIN *(runs up and takes hold of the machine, burning his hands)*

Don't give up now, boys! Only ten or twelve steps to go. Damn! It's hot as the flames of hell! *(Jerks away his burned hand.)*

CHUDAKOV

We can't carry it any farther. It looks like there are only a few seconds left. Faster! If we can just make it to the landing! OK, put it down here!

(POBEDONOSIKOV *rushes out through the door, slams it behind him, then knocks. The door opens slightly, and* POLYA *can be seen.)*

POBEDONOSIKOV

Now, you won't get all wrought up, will you, honey-bun? You must remember, Polechka, what you *yourself* can best understand: that only your goodwill can straighten out our life. That is, my life.

POLYA

My goodwill? *Myself?* It's not funny!

POBEDONOSIKOV

By the way, I forgot to hide my gun. Here [*handing her the gun*]. I probably won't be needing it, so will you hide it for me? Remember, it's loaded, and to fire it all you have to do is release this safety catch. Well, good-bye, Polechka!

(Pulls the door shut, bends down, and listens at the keyhole. MEZALYANSOVA *appears at the bottom of the stairway.)*

MEZALYANSOVA

Are you coming, Funny-Bunny-Nose?[1]

POBEDONOSIKOV

Shush-sh-sh!

(A rumbling, an explosion, a shot. POBEDONOSIKOV *throws open the door and rushes into his apartment. On the lower landing, a blaze of fireworks. On the spot where the machine had been put down,* THE PHOSPHORESCENT WOMAN *appears, holding a scroll with the word* "MANDATE" *inscribed in glowing letters. General stupefaction.* OPTIMISTENKO *comes running in, pulling up his pants. He is wearing slippers over bare feet.)*

OPTIMISTENKO

Where? Who was it?

THE PHOSPHORESCENT WOMAN

Greetings, comrades! I am a delegate from the year 2030. I've been switched into your present time for twenty-four hours. It's only a short time, and there's a lot to do. Please check my credentials and inform yourselves.

OPTIMISTENKO *(rushes up to* THE PHOSPHORESCENT WOMAN

and looks through the Mandate, reading the text aloud in a rapid mumble)

"Institute of the Origins of the History of Communism. . . ." Check. "Fully accredited. . . ." Check. "Select the best. . . ." Yes, quite clear. ". . . to be transferred to the Age of Communism. . . ." What's going on here? Good Lord, what's going on?

(Runs up the stairs [with the Mandate.] POBEDONOSIKOV, *irritated, appears on the threshold.)*

Comrade Pobedonosikov, a delegate from the Top Level is here to see you.

*(*POBEDONOSIKOV *takes off his cap, puts down his suitcase, and with a rather puzzled expression, runs his eye over the Mandate; then quickly, with a wave of the hand, invites* THE PHOSPHORESCENT WOMAN *and* OPTIMISTENKO *into his apartment.)*

POBEDONOSIKOV *(to* OPTIMISTENKO, *in a whisper)*

Twist the tail of that telephone! Ring up you know who, and find out if this kind of thing is possible. Find out whether it's in line with Party ethics, and whether it's OK for an atheist to believe in such supernatural phenomena.

(To THE PHOSPHORESCENT WOMAN*)*

Naturally, I was already informed of this project, and I rendered all possible assistance. Your competent authorities acted very wisely in sending you to me. Our committee has been working on the problem, and as soon as we receive the policy directives we'll coordinate with you. Come right on in to my study! And please don't pay any attention to a certain petty bourgeois atmosphere you may notice. It's merely the result of a failure to coordinate unequal cultural levels in matrimony.

(To VELOSIPEDKIN*)*

Come on in! Haven't I always told you to come straight to me?

*(*POBEDONOSIKOV *holds open the door for* THE PHOSPHORESCENT WOMAN, *who is gradually cooling down and assuming a normal appearance. To* OPTIMISTENKO, *who has come running back.)*

Well, what did they say?

OPTIMISTENKO

They just laughed and said it was beyond the boundaries of human understanding.

POBEDONOSIKOV

Ah! Beyond the boundaries! That means we'll have to clear it with the Society for Cultural Relations Abroad. We'll have to analyze every tiny detail. Comrade Mezalyansova, our dictation is postponed. Come on up here for urgent overtime cultural relations.

CURTAIN

ACT V

Same set as for Act II, but in disorder. A sign reads: BUREAU FOR SELECTION AND TRANSFER TO THE AGE OF COMMUNISM. MEZALYANSOVA, BELVEDONSKY, *and* IVAN IVANOVICH *are seated along the wall.* OPTIMISTENKO *is functioning as the administrative secretary who receives petitioners.* POBEDONOSIKOV *enters, in a bad mood, carrying a briefcase in either hand.*[1]

OPTIMISTENKO

What's your problem, citizen?

POBEDONOSIKOV

Things just can't go on like this! I'll speak out on the subject yet! I'll write about it in the bulletin-board newspaper. I most certainly will! We must combat red tape and favoritism. I demand that you let me bypass the line!

OPTIMISTENKO

How could there possibly be any red tape just before tryouts and selection? There's no need for you to bother her. If you want to avoid the line, that's easy. The line will pass through, and then you can go on your own without any line.

POBEDONOSIKOV

But I have to see her right now!

OPTIMISTENKO

Right now? Fine, right now! Only your watch isn't coordinated with hers. You see, comrade, she has a different time system. But as soon as she tells me, you can go in right now.

POBEDONOSIKOV

There are all kinds of things I must get cleared up in

connection with this transfer: my salary, my living quarters, and so on.

OPTIMISTENKO

Damn it all! Now you just listen to me! I don't want to see you around here again, pestering a big government agency with your petty problems! We can't be bothered with trifles. The government is interested in big things: various kinds of Fordism, time machines, and so on.

IVAN IVANOVICH

Have you ever been in a waiting line? I'm in a waiting line now, for the first time. Most uninteresting!

(POBEDONOSIKOV'*s former office is full of people. All the excitement and disorder of combat conditions, as during the first days of the Revolution.* THE PHOSPHORESCENT WOMAN *is speaking.)*

THE PHOSPHORESCENT WOMAN

Comrades, our meeting today is rather rushed. But I'll be spending years with many of you, and I'll tell you many other details of our joyful experience. Almost immediately, when we learned of your experiment, our scientists went on continuous watch. They helped you a lot, anticipating your inevitable miscalculations and correcting them. You and we came toward each other like two crews of workmen digging a tunnel, until we met – today.

You yourselves can't see the greatness of what you are doing. To us it is more apparent: we know what has already been achieved. I was astonished when I saw your little apartments – the kind we haven't had for a long time but have carefully preserved in our museums. I was amazed when I saw those giants of earth and steel, the grateful memory and experience of which we still treasure as a model of communist achievement and communist living. And I recognized some young people in greasy work clothes whom you haven't even noticed yet, but whose names glitter, in our century, on plates of demonetized gold. It was not until today, as I looked around me on my brief survey flight, that I fully understood the strength of your will and the rumbling of the stormy upheaval here, which has developed so rapidly into our happiness and the joy of the entire planet. How delighted I was when I beheld, today, the bright letters tracing the legend of your struggle – a struggle against the entire armed world of parasites and enslavers. You have no time to step back from your work and admire both it and yourselves. But I am glad to tell you of your greatness.

CHUDAKOV

Forgive me, comrade, for interrupting you but we only have six hours left, counting by our time, and I need your last-minute instructions on the number of people to be sent, the year of destination, and the speed.

THE PHOSPHORESCENT WOMAN

Direction: infinity. Speed: one year per second. Destination: the year 2030. How many are to be sent, and who they will be, are unknown quantities. All we know is their destination. Here, their value is not evident. But from the future, the past is like the palm of one's hand. Those persons will be accepted whose names will be remembered one hundred years from now. All right, comrade. Who is coming with you?

FOSKIN

Me.

DVOYKIN

Me.

TROYKIN

Me.

THE PHOSPHORESCENT WOMAN

And where are the mathematicians for plans and supervision?

FOSKIN

Us.

DVOYKIN

Us.

TROYKIN

Us.

THE PHOSPHORESCENT WOMAN

What? But you're workmen. Are you mathematicians, too?

VELOSIPEDKIN

It's very simple. We're workmen, but we're also studying at college.

THE PHOSPHORESCENT WOMAN

For us it's simple. But I didn't know whether it would be simple for you to make the change from the assembly line to the control panel – from the file to the comptometer.

DVOYKIN

That's not the kind of changeover we made, comrade. First we made battleships, then incendiary bombs. When we'd finished with the bombs, we made bayonets. And when we'd finished making bayonets, we changed over to tractors. On top of all that, we were taking all kinds of college courses. Among us, too, there were lots of people who didn't believe it could be done. But we liquidated that lack of faith in the working class. When you were studying our period, you made a slight error. Were you by any chance thinking of last year?

THE PHOSPHORESCENT WOMAN

I can see now that with your lively and forward-looking mind, you can come straight into our ranks and our work.

VELOSIPEDKIN

That's just what we're afraid of, comrade. We'll get the machine under way, all right. And naturally, if the Party cell sends us, we'll go. But please – it would be better not to take us anywhere for the time being. Our shop has just gone over to continuous production, and it'll be very important and interesting to see whether we fulfill the five-year plan in four years.

THE PHOSPHORESCENT WOMAN

I can promise you only one thing. We'll stop over at the station for the year 1934 to get the information you want. But if there are many people like you around, we have the answer already.

CHUDAKOV

Let's go, boys!

(The waiting room. CHUDAKOV, VELOSIPEDKIN, DVOYKIN, TROYKIN, *and* FOSKIN *walk through rap-*

idly, comparing blueprints as they go. POBEDONOSIKOV *trots after* CHUDAKOV, *who waves him off.)*

POBEDONOSIKOV *(gesticulating, irked)*

Just imagine! A nobody named Chudakov took advantage of the fact that he invented some little machine, and made friends with that silly woman – that female exec – before I could. In general I'm still not convinced that this isn't simply a case of immorality and in general a sexological contact.[2] Sex and character! Yes, that's it!

(To OPTIMISTENKO*)*

Subordinate Comrade Optimistenko, you surely understand that my problem is of major importance. It involves a hundred-year official trip by an executive – namely, myself – at the head of an entire agency.

OPTIMISTENKO

But your trip hasn't been authorized.

POBEDONOSIKOV

What do you mean, not authorized? I've been busy since morning making out the travel authorization and the credentials.

OPTIMISTENKO

Yes, but you see, it hasn't been coordinated with the Commissariat of Transportation.

POBEDONOSIKOV

What does the Commissariat of Transportation have to do with it? That's sheer stupidity! After all, this isn't a train. In that machine, forty persons or eight horses can travel a whole year into the future in just one second.

OPTIMISTENKO

Rejected! Impractical! Anyway, who'd want to go on a trip like that knowing he's entitled to expenses for a hundred years but will only be paid for a few seconds?

*(*POBEDONOSIKOV*'s former office.)*

THE PHOSPHORESCENT WOMAN

Comrades –

POLYA

May I say a word? Please forgive me for intruding, but I have no hopes at all. What hopes could I have? It's ridiculous. But I just wanted an answer to one question:

What is socialism? Comrade Pobedonosikov told me a lot about socialism, but somehow it's just not funny.

THE PHOSPHORESCENT WOMAN

You won't have long to wait. You'll be making the trip with your husband and children.

POLYA

My *children?* That's a laugh! I don't have any children. My husband says that in our critical times it's better not to be tied down to such an uncritical element – or maybe he said "aliment."

THE PHOSPHORESCENT WOMAN

All right, then, you're not tied to any children. But surely you have many other ties, since you're living with your husband.

POLYA

Living? That makes me laugh! I don't live with my husband. He lives with other women who're his equal in mentality and development. It's not funny.

THE PHOSPHORESCENT WOMAN

Then why do you call him your husband?

POLYA

So everybody will think he's against immorality. That's a laugh!

THE PHOSPHORESCENT WOMAN

I see. Then he just takes care of you, sees that you have all you need. Is that it?

POLYA

Oh, sure! He sees that I get nothing! He says that my acquisition of a new dress – that's the way he talks – would compromise him in the eyes of his colleagues. What a laugh!

THE PHOSPHORESCENT WOMAN

It's not funny.

(The waiting room. POLYA *is walking through.)*

POBEDONOSIKOV

What – you here? Did you report me? Did you complain?

POLYA

Complain? That's a laugh!

POBEDONOSIKOV

You told her the important things, of course. How we marched together, shoulder to shoulder, toward the rising sun of communism? How we struggled against the old way of life? Women go for sentimentality. She must have liked that, eh?

POLYA

Together? That's hilarious.

POBEDONOSIKOV

Be careful, Polya! You mustn't stain my honor as a Party member with an outstanding record of seniority. You must remember Party ethics and not wash dirty linen in public – or, as we say, haul the garbage out of the hut. By the way, you'd better go to the hut – our apartment, I mean – to tidy things up and haul out the garbage. And while you're there, you can pack up my things, because I'm leaving. I'm opposed to pluralism,[3] so I'm going alone. I'll send for you when in general I send for relatives to come. Now run along home, Polya, or –

POLYA

What do you mean, "or"? It's not funny.

*(*POBEDONOSIKOV*'s former office)*

THE PHOSPHORESCENT WOMAN

The choice of your agency was a matter of chance, just as inventions seem to be a matter of chance. No doubt the best specimens are to be found at places where people like Troykin and Dvoykin work. But there's a construction project on almost every square inch of land here, and we could get first-rate people from all those places, too.

TYPIST

Can I go along?

THE PHOSPHORESCENT WOMAN

Do you work here?

TYPIST

Right now I'm not working anywhere.

THE PHOSPHORESCENT WOMAN

How is that?

TYPIST

They fired me.

THE PHOSPHORESCENT WOMAN

Why?

TYPIST

Because I painted lips, they told me.

THE PHOSPHORESCENT WOMAN

Whose lips?

TYPIST

My own.

THE PHOSPHORESCENT WOMAN

And you didn't do anything else?

TYPIST

I typed and took shorthand.

THE PHOSPHORESCENT WOMAN

Did you do it well?

TYPIST

Yes.

THE PHOSPHORESCENT WOMAN

Then why aren't you working anywhere?

TYPIST

They fired me.

THE PHOSPHORESCENT WOMAN

Why?

TYPIST

I painted lips.

THE PHOSPHORESCENT WOMAN

Whose lips?

TYPIST

I already told you – my own!

THE PHOSPHORESCENT WOMAN

What business was it of theirs?

TYPIST

They fired me.

THE PHOSPHORESCENT WOMAN

Why?

TYPIST

Because I painted lips, they said.

THE PHOSPHORESCENT WOMAN

Why did you?

TYPIST

Because if you don't, they won't give you a job in the first place.

THE PHOSPHORESCENT WOMAN

I don't understand it. If you'd used lipstick on somebody else – let's say, on people who came to the office for information – then they could have said you were interfering with business and offending visitors. But as it is –

TYPIST

Comrade, please forgive me for my lips! What can I do? I wasn't a heroine in the underground, and my nose is all freckled. The only way I can get people to notice me is to put my best lip forward. Can it be that where you come from, people will notice a girl even if she doesn't use lipstick? If that's true, then give me a look at that life there – or even a tiny part of it! Of course, where you come from, everybody is important, with a distinguished record. They're all Pobedonosikovs of one kind or another, and they won't even notice me. But take me along anyway. . . . If I don't make the grade, I'll come back. . . . But please send me right now. On the way, I can do some kind of work. You can dictate your impressions to me, or maybe an expense report, and I'll type it up.

NOCHKIN

And I'll check the figures! It would be better for me, I've decided, to make my report to the Moscow DA's office in your century. Otherwise, while my case is still being looked into here –

(The waiting room.)

POBEDONOSIKOV

Write it down! Enter it in the record! In such a case I must state that I disclaim all responsibility! And if, as a result of unfamiliarity with the previous correspondence, and of poor selection of personnel, there should be a catastrophe –

OPTIMISTENKO

That's enough! Don't you dare threaten a big government agency! It's not proper to get us all worked up and nervous! And if a catastrophe *does* occur, we'll report to the police so they can draw up *their* record – a record of evidence!

(NOCHKIN *tries to pass through the room, hiding behind the* TYPIST.)

POBEDONOSIKOV (*ignoring* NOCHKIN *and looking hard at the* TYPIST)

What? You're still here at the agency? You're still at large? Comrade Optimistenko, why weren't the proper steps taken?

(*To the* TYPIST)

On the other hand, considering that you're still free, you can't refuse emergency work. In connection with my official trips it will be necessary to fill out the forms for travel expenses and per diem expenses, based on the normal concept of time and my average salary for one hundred years.

And then, of course, there'll be the special transportation expenses and the special expense account for official trips. Also, in case the machine breaks down, we may have to lay over at some backwoods half-year point for twenty or thirty years. All these things must be taken into account. We can't just go rolling off in a disorganized manner.

NOCHKIN

Why don't you just roll out of here like a salami in an organized manner?

(*Hides again.*)

IVAN IVANOVICH

A salami? Have you been to conferences? *I've* been to conferences. Nothing but salami and ham and cheese sandwiches everywhere! Most interesting!

[*Exits, together with* NOCHKIN *and the* TYPIST.]

POBEDONOSIKOV (*alone, collapsing into an armchair*)

Well, all right then, I'll quit! If they're going to treat me like this, I'll just say I'm retiring. Later on, they can study my life on the basis of portraits and the memoirs of my contemporaries. Yes, I'm quitting. But for you, comrades, things will be even worse!

(THE PHOSPHORESCENT WOMAN *comes out of the office.*)

OPTIMISTENKO

No more interviews today! Come back tomorrow and line up in the same order.

THE PHOSPHORESCENT WOMAN

What interviews? What tomorrow? What lineup?

OPTIMISTENKO *(pointing to the sign reading:* "IF YOU HAVEN'T BEEN ANNOUNCED, DON'T COME IN!")

It's according to the basic regulations.

THE PHOSPHORESCENT WOMAN

So you forgot to take down that stupid sign?

POBEDONOSIKOV *(jumping up and walking along beside* THE PHOSPHORESCENT WOMAN)

Greetings, comrade! Forgive me for coming late – awfully busy, you know. But I still wanted to drop in on you for a minute. You see, at first I declined to make the trip. But nobody would hear of it. "Go," they said, "and represent us!" Well, since the collective had asked me, I had to agree. But you must bear in mind, comrade, that I'm a top-level executive. It's all right for others to be treated like kolkhoz farmers if they want to, but not me! So take that into account beforehand, and get in touch with your people. Comrade Optimistenko can send a priority cable at our expense. Of course you understand that I must be offered a position corresponding to my seniority and official standing as the top executive in my field.

THE PHOSPHORESCENT WOMAN

Comrade, I never assign anybody anywhere. I came here only to convince you people of our existence. But don't worry – you'll be treated as you deserve to be.

POBEDONOSIKOV

You came incognito? I see! But between you and me, as persons charged with a mutual trust, there can be no secrets. And as a senior comrade I must warn you that you are surrounded by people who are not fully one-hundred-percent reliable. Velosipedkin smokes. Chudakov drinks – probably in proportion to his fantasies. And as for my wife, I must tell you – since I dare not conceal anything from the Party organization – that she is a petty bourgeois and addicted to new love affairs, new skirts, and everything we call the old way of life.

THE PHOSPHORESCENT WOMAN

What business is it of yours? For all that, they work –

POBEDONOSIKOV

What do you mean, "for all that"? I'm "for all that," too. But for all that, I don't drink, I don't smoke, I don't give tips, I don't lean toward the Left, I don't show up late for appointments, I don't

(bending down toward her ear)

indulge in excesses, I don't spare myself on the job, I –

THE PHOSPHORESCENT WOMAN

No matter what you talk about, it's always "I don't," "I don't," "I don't." Isn't there anything you "do, do, do"?

POBEDONOSIKOV

"Do, do, do"? Yes, there is. I implement directives, I file resolutions, I pay my Party dues, I receive my Party maximum salary, I sign papers, I stamp them with the official seal. . . . Yes, it's a regular little nook of socialism. No doubt where you come from the routing of documents is well organized – with a conveyor belt, right?

THE PHOSPHORESCENT WOMAN

I don't know what you're talking about. But of course the newsprint for the papers is fed into the presses very efficiently.

(Enter PONT KICH *and* MEZALYANSOVA.*)*

PONT KICH

Ahem! Ahem!

MEZALYANSOVA

Please, sir!

PONT KICH

Aseyev, hippopotamus, lend me, smashed-up face, and the cost was cut, May, thirty-six pounds, watchification.[4]

MEZALYANSOVA

Mr. Pont Kich is trying to tell you that in view of the complete uselessness of watches, he can buy them all up at a fair government price, and then he'll believe in communism.

THE PHOSPHORESCENT WOMAN

We can understand that even without a translation.

[And the answer is] first recognize us — [5] then you'll get your profits! Comrades, be here on the dot! The first time-train leaves promptly at twelve o'clock for the year 2030!

CURTAIN

ACT VI

CHUDAKOV's basement. CHUDAKOV, VELOSIPEDKIN, and DVOYKIN are busying themselves around the invisible machine. THE PHOSPHORESCENT WOMAN is checking it against a blueprint. TROYKIN is guarding the door.

THE PHOSPHORESCENT WOMAN

Comrade Foskin, you can put on ordinary windshields. The five-year plan has accustomed you people to the rhythm and speed. The transition will hardly be noticeable.

FOSKIN

I'll change the glass. Half-millimeter. Unbreakable.

THE PHOSPHORESCENT WOMAN

Comrade Dvoykin, check the springs. See to it there's no jouncing when we hit the bumps and potholes of holidays. Continuous production has spoiled all of us with smooth going.

DVOYKIN

The going will be smooth, all right – unless vodka bottles are scattered along the way.

THE PHOSPHORESCENT WOMAN

Comrade Velosipedkin, check the discipline gauge! It will detect any offenders, and they'll be thrown overboard.

VELOSIPEDKIN

No problem. We'll keep a taut ship.

THE PHOSPHORESCENT WOMAN

Comrade Chudakov, are we ready to go?

CHUDAKOV

Let's mark out the position, and then the passengers can come aboard.

(A white ribbon is unrolled from a spool and

stretched out between the wheels of the invisible machine.)

VELOSIPEDKIN

All right, Troykin, let's go!

(From all directions, passengers carrying placards crowd forward to the tune of "The March of Time.")

The March of Time

Rise up and soar,
O song of mine,
As Red troops
swing along!
March
on-
ward,
Time!
O
Time,
march on!
Quicken your pace,
dear land of mine,
Old ways
are dead
and gone!
March
on-
ward,
Time!
O
Time,
march on!
Yet faster still,
dear land of mine —
Ahead lies
the commune!
March
on-
ward,
Time!

O
Time,
march on!
Five years are planned for –
bonuses
Will
cut them short by one!
March
on-
ward,
Time!
O
Time,
march on!
Make factories hum
dear land of mine
All day and all night long!
March
on-
ward,
Time
O
Time,
march on!
Strike harder yet,
commune of mine,
Till evil ways
are gone!
March
on-
ward,
Time!
O
Time,
march on!
Rise up and soar,
O song of mine,
As Red troops
swing along!

March
on-
ward,
Time!
O
Time,
march on!

OPTIMISTENKO *(stepping out of the crowd; to* CHUDAKOV*)*

Comrade, I must ask you something confidentially. Will there be a diner? No? Just as I thought! Why wasn't a directive issued on the subject? They forgot, did they? Oh, well, there'll be enough to drink. And as for food, we'll make ends meet. Just come to our compartment. Where is it, by the way?

CHUDAKOV

Stand in line, all of you! Shoulder to shoulder! And don't worry about getting tired. One turn of this wheel, and within a second —

POBEDONOSIKOV *(entering, with* MEZALYANSOVA*)*

They haven't sounded the "all aboard" signal yet? Well, they can go ahead now, and then sound the second one right away.

(To DVOYKIN*)*

Comrade, are you a Party member? Yes? Well, just for friendship's sake, and quite unofficially, give us a hand with those bags, will you? They contain some important papers — very important! I couldn't entrust them to a non-Party redcap who carried bags just for money. But with you, a promoted worker, it's different. . . . *Bring them along, please!* . . . You I can trust. Now, who's in charge of seating arrangements here? Where is my compartment? Naturally, I'll have a lower bunk.

THE PHOSPHORESCENT WOMAN

The time machine is not fully outfitted yet. As pioneers in this kind of transportation, you two will have to stand up along with the rest.

POBEDONOSIKOV

What do Pioneers have to do with it? The Pioneer Rally[1] is over. I must ask you not to bother me with any more of that Pioneer stuff! This campaign is over! I just won't go! What the hell is this, anyway? It's time people learned how to treat a member of the Old Guard. If they don't, I'll retire from the Guard. And, finally, I demand compensation for my unutilized vacation. In short, where are my bags?

(DVOYKIN *enters, pushing a baggage cart loaded with bales of documents, hatboxes, briefcases, hunting rifles, and* MEZALYANSOVA'*s wardrobe trunk. Sitting on the four corners of the handcart are four Irish setters. Behind it comes* BELVEDONSKY *with a suitcase, a paintbox, and a portrait.*)

THE PHOSPHORESCENT WOMAN

Comrade, what is this? A department store?

OPTIMISTENKO

Not at all – just a little accumulation.

THE PHOSPHORESCENT WOMAN

But why do you need it? You'll have to leave at least part of it behind.

OPTIMISTENKO [*to* POBEDONOSIKOV]

Of course, comrade, you can have the rest sent on by mail.

POBEDONOSIKOV

No comments, please! Hang up a bulletin-board newspaper, and print your comments there! I'll have to submit circular letters, authorizations, copies, theses, second copies, corrections, excerpts, references, card files, resolutions, reports, minutes of proceedings, and other certifying documents even for these materially evident dogs. I *could* ask for a private car, but in accordance with my modest scale of living, I won't. Never lose sight of long-range policy! You, too, will find it comes in very handy. When I've got my staff, I'll shift my agency to a worldwide scale. Then, when I've expanded my staff, I'll shift it to the interplanetary scale. I trust you don't want to debureaucratize and disorganize the planet?

OPTIMISTENKO (*to* THE PHOSPHORESCENT WOMAN)

Don't raise any objections, citizen. It's too bad, though, for the planet.

THE PHOSPHORESCENT WOMAN

All right, but get a move on!

POBEDONOSIKOV

I must ask you not to interfere in matters over which you have no authority! You've gone too far! I must ask you not to forget that these people are my personnel; and so long as I haven't been fired, I'm top executive here! I've had enough! The moment I seize the reins of power in my new post, I'm going to register complaints with everybody about absolutely all of you! One side, comrades! Put my bags down there! And where is my light-yellow calfskin briefcase with my monogram on it? Optimistenko, run back and get it! Don't worry – they'll wait. I'm delaying the departure of this train for reasons of the national interest – not just for some trifle.

(OPTIMISTENKO *starts to rush out, and meets up with* POLYA, *carrying the briefcase.*)

POLYA

Please don't get all excited! I was tidying up the apartment, as you told me to – and I'm going back right now to finish the job. But I saw something I thought you'd forgotten. It looked important, I thought. What a laugh! So I came running with it. Here you are!

(Hands him the briefcase.)

POBEDONOSIKOV

I'll take the briefcase, and I'll take your story under consideration. But you should remind me of these things beforehand. The next time this happens I shall consider it a breach and weakening of marital discipline. *All visitors leave the ship!* Good-bye, Polya. When I'm settled, I'll send you a third of whatever it is, in accordance with the practice of the court and until such time as that obsolete legislation has been changed.

PONT KICH *(entering and stopping)*

Ahem! Ahem!

MEZALYANSOVA

Please, sir!

PONT KICH

The impudent thief stripped jasmine from the linden trees. Give us. Spit! Ticketnik.[2]

MEZALYANSOVA

Mr. Pont Kich wants to say, and does say, that he has

no ticket because he didn't know which kind he should get: a Party card or a railroad ticket. But he is willing to grow into any kind of socialism, just so it's profitable to him.

OPTIMISTENKO

Please, sir! We can reach an agreement en route.

IVAN IVANOVICH

Greetings! Our greetings to you and your and our achievements! Just one more effort, boys, and we'll overcome all that. Have you seen socialism? I'm about to see socialism. Most interesting!

POBEDONOSIKOV

And so, comrades. . . . Why and where did we stop?

TYPIST

We stopped on "And so, comrades. . . ."

POBEDONOSIKOV

Oh, yes! I demand the floor. I am taking the floor! And so, comrades, we are living through an age when, in my administrative apparatus, an apparatus of time has been invented. This apparatus of liberated time was invented in my apparatus, and nowhere else, because in my apparatus there was as much free time as you could want. The present, current moment is characterized by the fact that it is a stationary moment. And since, in a stationary moment, we do not know where the beginning ends and where the end begins, at the beginning I shall say a few concluding words, and then a few beginning ones.

A fine apparatus,
One I'm glad to see!
We're so glad – both me
And my apparatus!

We are glad because, once we go on vacation once a year, and don't let the year move ahead, we can go on vacation two years out of every year. And, on the other hand, whereas now we get paid once a month, once we make a month go by in one day we can get paid every day of the month. And so, comrades –

VOICES

Away with him!

Can it!
No more prayers – let's get going!
Chudakov, switch off his time!

*(*CHUDAKOV *turns off* POBEDONOSIKOV, *who continues to gesticulate but is heard by no one.)*

OPTIMISTENKO

In my turn, I am taking the floor in the name of all of us, personally.

[*To* POBEDONOSIKOV]

And I'll tell you person to person, without respect of persons, that it doesn't matter to us what person heads the agency, because we respect only that person who is put there and continues to head it. But let me say impersonally that to each of us personally it is a pleasure that you, with your pleasant personality, are once again chief. Therefore, in the name of all of us, personally, I present you with this watch, since this ticking timepiece will be perfectly suitable to you, personally, as the person at the head of –

VOICES

Away with him!
Pickle his tongue!
Chudakov, turn him off!

*(*CHUDAKOV *turns off* OPTIMISTENKO, *who likewise goes on gesticulating although nobody hears him.)*

THE PHOSPHORESCENT WOMAN

Comrades! At the first signal we'll rush ahead, breaking through the old, decrepit time. The future will accept anyone who possesses even one trait making him kin to the collective of the commune: joy in working, eagerness to make sacrifices, unwearying creativeness, willingness to share advantages, pride in being human. Our five-year strides will be continued and multiplied tenfold. Keep together in a huddle – tighter! Fleet time will sweep off and overboard all ballast made heavy by trash – also the ballast of those made empty by disbelief.

POBEDONOSIKOV

Stand back, Polya!

NOCHKIN *(runs up, pursued)*

All I want is to reach socialism. They'll judge my case there!

POLICEMAN *(catching up, blows his whistle)*

Stop that man!

(An explosion, with pale-blue light. "The March of Time." Darkness. Left on the stage, knocked flat and sprawling by the devilish wheel of time, are POBEDONOSIKOV, OPTIMISTENKO, BELVEDONSKY, PONT KICH, *and* IVAN IVANOVICH.*)*

OPTIMISTENKO

We're there! Let's get out!

POBEDONOSIKOV

Polya! Polechka! Feel me! Examine me thoroughly! I think I've been run over by time. Polina! . . . Did they take her away? Arrest them! Overtake and surpass them![3] What time is it?

(Looks at his gift watch.)

OPTIMISTENKO

Give it back! Give that watch back, citizen! A plain, everyday bribe isn't suitable to you, personally, especially since I – in the name of all of us, personally – put a whole month's salary into that watch! We'll find another person to respect and give watches to.

IVAN IVANOVICH

You have to break eggs to make an omelet. The little – the big defects of the mechanism. I must go and beguile the Soviet public. Most interesting!

POBEDONOSIKOV

Artist, seize this opportunity and paint a living man mortally offended!

BELVEDONSKY

Oh, no! Something has gone wrong with the foreshortening in your case. An artist must look up to his model, like a duck looking up at a balcony. I can get good artistic results only when I'm looking up from below.

POBEDONOSIKOV *(to* MEZALYANSOVA*)*

OK! OK! Let them go ahead and try. Let them navigate "leaderless, and without sails."[4] I'll retire to private life and write my memoirs. Let's go, the two of us together – you and me, your Funny-Bunny-Nose.

MEZALYANSOVA

I already have a nose, and it's out of joint. Very badly out of joint, in fact. You couldn't set up socialism, and you couldn't set up a woman, either! Oh, you're an impressive little miniature of a man, I must say! *Good-bye! Adieu! Auf Wiedersehen! Proschayte!* Come, my Kichi, my Ponchi-Kichi-koo!

(Exits with PONT KICH.*)*

POBEDONOSIKOV

She, and you, and the author – all of you! What have you been trying to say here? That people like me aren't of any use to communism?

CURTAIN

1930

NOTES

Vladimir Mayakovsky, A Tragedy

1. A play on the idiom *popast' pal'tsem v nebo* (literally: "to stick one's finger into the sky"), meaning to make a bad blunder.

Mystery-Bouffe

CHARACTERS

1. The list of Dramatis Personae in the original is incomplete, since it does not include either the personification of Chaos or such minor characters carelessly retained from the First Version as The Shoemaker and The Chimney Sweep.
2. I.e., a Menshevik.

PROLOGUE

1. In *Mystery-Bouffe* the action at times involves other areas of the theater in addition to the stage.

ACT I

1. An allusion to Philipp Scheidemann, leader of the German Social Democratic Party and briefly (in 1919) Chancellor of the Provisional Government of Germany, who was considered by the Bolsheviks to be a "traitor to the working class."
2. The Cheka – a portmanteau word for the formidable designation: All-Russian Extraordinary Commission for Combating Counterrevolution and Sabotage – was exactly that.
3. In the original, *intelligent,* or even *intelligentsia.* (In the First Version he was simply called "a student.")
4. In the original, *po Kautskomy;* i.e., in accordance with the thinking of Karl Kautsky, a German Marxist of decidedly more moderate leanings than the Bolsheviks.
5. Some of the lines spoken by the Compromiser are, like these, lifted bodily from speeches of the Hysterical Lady of the First Version. Hence their overly sharp edge of hysteria. (Cf. Clemenceau's lines, immediately following.)
6. Cf. Note 3, above.

ACT II

1. It is difficult (as it often is in Mayakovsky's plays) to tell to whom this line applies. In any case, "sea dog" would have been perhaps more accurate; but the "wolf" had to be kept for the sake of the Farmhand's pun a few lines later.
2. In the First Version, these lines were spoken by the German Army Officer and the Italian Army Officer, who were armed. Cf. Note 3, below.
3. In the First Version, addressed by the Italian Army Officer to the German Lieutenant.
4. Another unwarranted retention from the First Version, where it was apparently addressed to the Hysterical Lady.
5. In the original, "October twenty-fifth" – the date of the Bolshevik Revolution according to the Old Style calendar.
6. In the original "Revolution isn't a young officer [Junker]." Another retention from the First Version, where it was addressed to the Hysterical Lady, who responded with the bite on the arm immediately following. Cf. Note 5 to Act I.
7. An allusion to Krylov's fable "The Monkey and the Spectacles."

ACT III

1. In the First Version, the stage directions describe Hell as consisting of three layers of smoky-yellow clouds. The top layer was Purgatory, and the middle one, Hell. Some of the action in Act III makes no sense without reference to these stage directions.
2. A reference to the rationing categories employed during the Civil War and after.
3. Cf. Note 1, above.
4. Cf. Note 1, above.

ACT IV

1. These words occur in the Russian, not the English, translation of the "Internationale."
2. General Wrangel, a commander of White forces opposing the Bolsheviks in the Civil War.

ACT V

1. A Soviet scholar, F. Pitskel, in his notes to a three-volume edition of Mayakovsky's works (Moscow, 1965), points out that the Soldier voices the views advanced by Trotsky, and opposed by Lenin, in the big Party fracas over trade-union policies in 1920–21. For that matter, so does the Miner, since Trotsky favored "appointed officials" as opposed to elected ones.

2. More trade-union politics. Bukharin, Pitskel tells us, supported a "buffer platform" by way of reconciling Trotsky and Lenin.
3. The Don Basin is Russia's largest coal-producing region.
4. An allusion to the fact that black-marketeers, during the Civil War, often hopped freight trains for free rides with their sacks of products.
5. Cf. Note 1 to Act IV.

ACT VI

1. An industrial town.
2. Ditto.
3. The Russian word for hospitality is "bread-salt."
4. This refers to Lenin's New Economic Policy (NEP), advocating "learning from the bourgeois how to do business."
5. This "chorale" is Mayakovsky's own adaptation of the Russian version of the "Internationale."

The Bedbug

CHARACTERS

1. Many of the characters listed here are not to be found among the Dramatis Personae as listed by Mayakovsky. In this play, as elsewhere, he seems to enjoy letting his characters pop up unannounced, as though in deliberate defiance of that favorite sign of the bureaucrats that he loathed so much: IF YOU HAVEN'T BEEN ANNOUNCED, DON'T COME IN! The locale of Scenes I–IV is Tambov; the time, 1929.
2. The name Skripkin comes from the Russian for "violin" (*skripka*), an instrument emblematic for Mayakovsky of petty bourgeois sentimentalism.
3. A dig at those hack journalists of the early twenties who were fond of likening the capitalism of the NEP (New Economic Policy) to a "Russian Renaissance."
4. Bayan was a legendary Russian bard.

SCENE I

1. General Umberto Nobile, Italian explorer whose dirigible crashed after a flight over the North Pole in 1928. The survivors were rescued by a Russian icebreaker.
2. The first mention of the new name chosen by Prisypkin as fitting for his new way of life. Henceforth he is called by both names — sometimes Prisypkin, sometimes Skripkin.
3. In the original, "Mr. Ryabushinsky" — a well-known millionaire.

4. In archaic Russian, the word for "red" (*krasny*) also means "beautiful"; hence, "Red Square," etc.
5. Georgi Plekhanov, a leading Marxist theoretician.
6. An admirable custom at Russian weddings. When the guests cry "Bitter!" the bride and groom kiss, thereby making the guests' vodka sweeter.
7. Mayakovsky is here reproducing, only slightly varied, a stupid bit of doggerel by a would-be poet, one I. N. Molchanov, celebrating his jilting of a girl friend, which appeared in *Komsomolskaya Pravda.* My own version is rather free, in the Lowellesque manner.

SCENE II

1. A minor poet of the late nineteenth century heartily disliked by Mayakovsky.
2. Ditto, except that Nadson was better than Apukhtin.
3. In the original, "Do you think you're Karl Liebknecht?" Liebknecht was a German socialist much admired in Soviet Russia.
4. In the original, "nepmen's daughters." The "nepmen" were entrepreneurs who prospered [(most of them, anyway)] under the New Economic Policy in the twenties.
5. This cryptic line presumably refers to psychological warfare being waged against the Bolsheviks.
6. See following note.
7. These two stanzas are from the poem Mayakovsky addressed to I. N. Molchanov's jilted girl friend. Cf. Note 7. Scene I.
8. So literally – for the sake of the gruesome pun. But the Russian phrase means the opposite of the English; i.e., "not with a bang but a whimper."

SCENE III

1. Perekop – a city in the Crimea. The battle in question was fought in late 1920, and resulted in the White forces' being driven out of the Crimea.
2. Vera Kholodnaya was an actress in the early days of motion pictures. Sasha Makarov was a composer of "romances," or love laments.

SCENE IV

1. Alexander Zharov – a Communist poet detested by Mayakovsky.

SCENE VI

1. I. P. Utkin, a poet of sorts, and a contemporary of Mayakovsky, wrote a poem called "The Guitar," which Mayakovsky considered intolerably saccharine.

SCENE IX

1. Literally, "by Bebel." Quite apart from the suggestion of the Bible, the Tower of Babel, etc., August Bebel is here specifically intended. He was one of the founders of the German Social Democratic Party.

2. Riding breeches (and boots) were a status symbol of the big operators in the post-Revolutionary period.

The Bathhouse

CHARACTERS

1. Most of the names corresponding to "humors" are easily recognizable cognates; e.g., Optimistenko, Mezalyansova (from *mésalliance*), etc., including the suggestion of "kitsch" in Pont Kich. The only exceptions of any importance are:

Pobedonosikov – "nose for victory," with a connotation of "overbearing."

Chudakov – from *chudak,* meaning "an eccentric." But the root word, *chudo,* means "miracle," so that the inventor's name indicates something more than a mere eccentric.

2. All-Union Society for Cultural Relations with Foreign Countries.

ACT I

1. In the original, "more useless than an ox in the Avtodor," the latter being a portmanteau word with the improbable expansion: "All-Union Society for the Furthering of Automobile Transportation, the Tractor Industry, and Road Construction."

2. One P. S. Kogan, no great friend of Mayakovsky, was then president of the National Academy of Artistic Sciences.

3. "Do you speak English?" Mezalyansova actually puts the question in kind of a schoolgirl English, which she uses elsewhere in phrases like "Please, sir!" Just this once, to help create the multilingual confusion Mayakovsky intended, I have reversed her English into Russian.

4. Ivan Ivanovich here confuses Friedrich Engels with the title of a famous treatise written by Engels (in partial collaboration with Marx), and Liverpool with Manchester, where Engels lived for much of his life.

5. The basic watchdog group for "public control" of government agencies and industry. Abbreviation: RKI.

6. In the original, "Anatol Vasil'ch" – meaning Anatol Vasilyevich Lunacharsky, the literary critic who served for twelve years as Commissar for Education.

7. Throughout, Pont Kich speaks a weird kind of Mayakovskian

English expressed through Russian words in jumbled syntax, rather on the analogy of "fractured" French. Decoding back to the dubious "English" original is largely a matter of guesswork – and Mezalyansova's erratic interpreting doesn't help much. (Not that it really matters.) Roughly reconstructed, the line in question comes out something like: "I want very well . . . ah . . . very badly . . . I shall try 'em again. I do not understand. Peer, he, Purchill [Churchill?]. Oh, he's very invention."

8. Decoded version: "That's all right. I'm very, very lazy and I shall to go. Do you want gold rubles?"

9. "Private" was of course a word of abuse, although private enterprise had been authorized under Lenin's New Economic Policy earlier in the twenties.

ACT II

1. I.e., "Pashka Tigerpaw."

2. A sly allusion to the fact that the "self-criticism" encouraged by Party ideologues commonly turned out, in practice, to be criticism of others.

3. A pun on the title of Tolstoy's comedy *The Fruits of Education* (or *Enlightenment*, or *Culture* – since the key word, *prosveshcheniye*, means any of the three).

4. Pobedonosikov makes three elementary boners in this line. Pushkin's full name was Alexander Sergeyevich Pushkin; *Eugene Onegin* is a "novel in verse," not a play; and the opera based on it was, of course, composed by Tchaikovsky.

5. A Soviet editor of Mayakovsky's works, G. Cheremina, has pointed out that there was indeed a famous family of French cabinetmakers with the name of Jacob, but that none of them bore the first name Louis.

6. There is some complicated punning going on here, as a result of Pobedonosikov's being made addlepated by rage, based on the phrase "immediate, responsible." One dropped prefix, one wrong suffix, and the shade of Karl Marx becomes "mediocre" and "irresponsible."

7. A variation on two lines from Krylov's fable "The Dragonfly and the Ant":

> . . . When under every little leaf
> Both bed and board awaited her.

ACT III

1. An instance of Mayakovsky's well-known laxity in stage directions (less pronounced in this play, however, than elsewhere). Pobedonosikov's line, and Mezalyansova's answer, make sense only

if we assume the presence of Pont Kich, stuffed with caviar and perhaps snoozing somewhere in a corner.

2. A more or less literal rendering of Pobedonosikov's confused Russian verbiage.

3. An adaptation to the bureaucratic milieu and mentality of four famous lines from Lermontov's narrative poem *The Demon*:

The hour of tryst, the hour of parting,
Brings them neither joy nor grief.
They hope for nothing from the future,
For them the past holds no regrets.

4. More fractured language, playing on the German words for "eleven" and "twelve" (*elf* and *zwölf*).

5. I.e., the maximum salary that a Party member could receive.

6. In the original, "The Soviet day, the Party day/Of a bu-reaucrat."

7. From the Russian version of the "Internationale."

8. More rudimentary boners. Ivan Ivanovich confounds Chekhov's *The Cherry Orchard* and *Uncle Vanya* with Katayev's *The Squaring of the Circle* and Bulgakov's *The Days of the Turbines.*

ACT IV

1. In the original, *Nosik* or "Little Nose" — from Pobedo*nosik*ov. Cf. Mezalyansova's parting words to him in Act VI.

ACT V

1. More careless stage directions. Mayakovsky has Pobedonosikov, at one and the same time, sitting on the bench along the wall with the others, and entering. In our version, he has been removed from the bench.

2. In the original, ". . . a contact of the Friedland type." The reference is to Dr. L. Friedland's book, published in 1927: *Behind Closed Doors: the Notes of a Venerologist.*

3. *Sovmestitelstvo* — holding two positions at one time. The root meaning is "sharing a place" — hence Pobedonosikov's unintentional pun.

4. In Mayakovskian English, as nearly as I can reconstruct it: "I say, if big enough, dive dog! The League is beat! History must sneeze. He lost my poodle. Watchification. . . ."

5. At the time when *The Bathhouse* was completed (September, 1929) Great Britain had not yet renewed its earlier (and subsequently revoked) diplomatic recognition of the Soviet Union.

ACT VI

1. A pun on the word *slët,* which means both "rally" and (more basically) "flight."
2. Decoded version: "Worn out. I'll sleep. Just mine. Dine [on?] plenty. Be later."
3. "Overtake and surpass" (American industrial production) – a common propaganda slogan.
4. A mutilation of another line from Lermontov's *The Demon*:

   Rudderless, and without sails. . . .